T0147392

———— ALSO BY DON AMBROSE ————

- Imagitronics

- Creative Intelligence: Toward Theoretic Integration

- Expanding Visions of Creative Intelligence: An Interdisciplinary Approach

- Morality, Ethics, and Gifted Minds

Scoundrels, Thugs, and Fools

—— Adventures in Neoconland ——

Don Ambrose

iUniverse, Inc.
New York   Bloomington

Scoundrels, Thugs, and Fools
Adventures in Neoconland

Copyright © 2009 by Don Ambrose

All rights reserved. No part of this book may be used or reproduced by any means, graphic, electronic, or mechanical, including photocopying, recording, taping or by any information storage retrieval system without the written permission of the publisher except in the case of brief quotations embodied in critical articles and reviews.

iUniverse books may be ordered through booksellers or by contacting:

iUniverse
1663 Liberty Drive
Bloomington, IN 47403
www.iuniverse.com
1-800-Authors (1-800-288-4677)

Because of the dynamic nature of the Internet, any Web addresses or links contained in this book may have changed since publication and may no longer be valid. The views expressed in this work are solely those of the author and do not necessarily reflect the views of the publisher, and the publisher hereby disclaims any responsibility for them.

ISBN: 978-1-4401-1783-1 (pbk)
ISBN: 978-1-4401-1784-8 (ebk)

Printed in the United States of America

iUniverse rev. date: 2/24/09

Special thanks to Janet Stern, Senior Copyeditor, for helpful improvements to the content; to Brian Ambrose for designing the cover and refining the graphics; and to Carmina Alvarez-Gaffin, Senior Book Designer, and Marcella Roberts, Book Designer, for additional schematic recommendations

Contents

List of Figures and Tables

A PREVIEW OF YOUR JOURNEY

Say hello to an angry, bombastic, venom-spewing, talk-show pundit; a scrawny, wild-eyed, psychopathic news commentator; a spoiled, dull-witted, blue-blooded heir to a fortune; and a burly, aggressive, sadistic prison warden. They have something in common. In addition to an extremely self-centered approach to life, they're all neoconservatives you'll meet on this adventurous journey through a not-so-far-away, utopian, island nation. Inspired by Jonathan Swift's elegantly refined satire in *Gulliver's Travels;* Bill Maher's biting, comedic, political critiques; and the exquisitely uproarious intellectual slapstick of John Stewart and Stephen Colbert in their fake-news programs, this is an attempt at sociopolitical satire during a time when it is desperately needed. It is a story about a trip through the imaginary nation of Neoconland, which is dominated thoroughly by neoconservatives much like those who grace us with their domineering presence in the good old USA. It is a thought experiment of sorts based on the question "What would it be like if neoconservatives came to control a nation completely and pushed their belief system to the extreme?" Some would say a few nations in today's world already have brought this thought experiment to fruition, and these arguments would be hard to refute.

As you'll see on your journey through Neoconland, the behaviors of its citizens are bizarre and can make you laugh and weep simultaneously. This story highlights these perplexing behaviors in the hope that we can recognize and reverse some disturbing, damaging trends the real-world neocons have foisted upon us. You'll find the characters irritating, ridiculous, and hilarious at times. You also might perceive some interesting similarities between them and some real people of prominence in today's political, economic, cultural, and media worlds. Of course, any resemblances are entirely coincidental, and the intent is not to make fun of people gratuitously. Not all neoconservatives are vile, ignorant, or brutish, and some of them are good friends of mine. Well, maybe not *good* friends, but there certainly are neocons I like and respect. Moreover, in spite of its extremist, misguided dogma, there's good to be found in the ideology itself with its emphasis on individual freedom, innovation, and creative self-actualization. But the damage done by neoconservatives is evident in the exploitation of the working poor at home and in sweatshops abroad, the destruction of the environment, the erosion of civil liberties, and the arrogance of international conquest in Iraq and elsewhere.

How can ordinary, good-hearted people blindly follow a belief system that's been so destructive in recent decades? Perhaps any ideology taken too far, regardless of its initial merits, can become oppressive. That's what happened to conservatism. A large branch of it mutated into neoconservatism, which became a runaway system, an ideology run amok, a snorting, raging economic bull in a globalized china shop.

For about two decades now I've reacted to ever-increasing neoconservative excesses with a mixture of bemusement, irritation, disbelief, and anger, with the disbelief and anger dominating since the turn of the 21st century when the Republican party achieved virtually unchecked control over the American political arena. The arrogant decadence of the neoconservative agenda eventually encouraged me to create this fable in an effort to shed some light on their abuses. I am mildly ashamed of myself for giving in to the writing of a book like this, which is highly critical and at times a little unfair. In self-defense, I did resist for about 15 years, for what that's worth, but one can only take so much. Neoconservative skullduggery, corruption, dogmatism, deception, and the wild spin of blatant propaganda finally drove me to create this window into Neoconland. Whatever parallels you draw between this story and the real world, I hope you will use them to recognize and work against some of the neocons' most harmful exploits.

Not that they haven't had critics, and some very effective ones at that. For example, in addition to Maher, Stewart, and Colbert, there have been comedic columns, books, and media appearances by Al Franken, Molly Ivins, Rachel Maddow, Keith Obermann, Jim Hightower, Thom Hartmann, and others; as well as the punchy exposés provided by Naomi Klein's revelations of our descent toward fascism, Michael Moore's documentaries and publications about various abusive and exploitative practices in the corporate world, and John Cusack's satirical movie about the corrupt profiteering in the Iraq war *(War, Inc.)*. Some courageous politicians have been swimming upstream against powerful ideological currents (e.g., Dennis Kucinich). On the more academic side there has been a large number of rigorous scholarly investigations from various academic disciplines revealing neoconservative excesses in the economic, political, and cultural dimensions of today's world. Some prominent scholars have found ways to extend their messages to larger lay audiences (e.g., Paul Krugman, Noam Chomsky). I use these critiques as background for the story, as described later in this introduction.

While these criticisms and revelations have been helpful, we need something a little different—something along the lines of a 21st-century *Gulliver's Travels:* a fable revealing the foolishness of neoconservative excesses complete with extraordinary, freakish characters, bizarre locations, and wacky events. This book conveys such a fable through the exploits of fantastic creatures including Gil Flounderfib, a human-fish hybrid who deposits ideological mind excrement in the bottom of neoconservative think tanks. You'll also meet an apeman by the name of Hear No Warnings—a cloning experiment gone awry and a deranged political regulator of any scientific research that doesn't fit the Neoconian corporate or moral agenda. Along with these strange creatures you'll meet Neoconians who are somewhat more human. Well, they are more human in physical form at least. For example, you'll visit with Hubris Mendacious, a long-serving politician who dances to the tune of corporate lobbyists whenever they vigorously pull his puppet strings, which are attached with metal eye hooks screwed into his knees, wrists, skull, larynx, and groin. In order to give you a closer look at these oddball characters, locations, and artifacts, I depict many of them in the form of cartoon drawings throughout the text.

There's one other thing that may take you by surprise when you arrive on Neoconian shores. You'll notice that the names of people, places, and artifacts reflect their personality and behavioral characteristics. For example, Howler Frenzy, the son of the most prominent televangelist in the nation, acts much like his name suggests. His sermons are both thunderous and maniacal, hence his prominence in the consciousness of the people. Hidebound Flimflam III Esquire, a famous fellow from a leading neoconservative think tank and the author of a book glorifying the sanitized history of the nation, is staunchly conservative (hidebound) and his writings are fraudulent (prone to flimflam). And of course you'll hear about the famous heiress and socialite Bimbo Jumbobazoom and the perky news reporter Britney Bubblehead. Their names mean—oh, you've probably guessed already. As for places, there are some large urban centers that reveal neoconservative excesses. The capital city, Fascisto, is named after the extremist, right-wing form of government the Neoconians tend to promote aggressively. The massive slum city of Toxica is an impoverished factory town full of destitute people, poisonous industrial effluent, decomposing carcasses, and other environmental toxins. The retail hub, Big Boxica, is the home of big-box superstores and the center of the materialistic universe. Speaking of materialism, while in Big Boxica you'll get to test drive an Earth Devastator, a 13-foot-high, road-hogging, pollution-spewing, gas-guzzling Excessive Egomobile. As you can tell from the vehicle model name, you'll crave one of these if you have a grossly over-inflated ego in constant need of massage.

There are many other astonishing things to see in Neoconland: everything from a television set that *watches you* very carefully to inspect your behavior as you flip through mind-numbing reality shows; to the Boneshredder assault rifle and fragmentation grenades that every child wants to see under the Christmas tree; to the electric skull drills the teachers use to enable the stuffing of small brains with meaningless triviabits; to the toxic-waste wrist tattoos that so readily identify the low-class, Putrid Scum so upper-class Splendiferous Bluebloods can exclude them from employment and social networks. I invite you to guess the hidden and not-so-hidden meanings behind the names of all the people, places, and things you'll confront on the trip. If you want to check your guesses, answers are provided in parentheses after most entries in the glossaries in the back.

Most effective fables or myths use the quirky exploits of mystifying characters to convey moral messages and this book attempts to accomplish the same. But it also goes beyond other fables by connecting the story solidly with present-day reality. The outlandish characters, events, and places in the story are here not just to entertain you, although I certainly hope they do. They're also intended to symbolize disturbing details about the strong neoconservative influence on the real world. For this reason, I provide extensive footnotes explaining the meaning of the story's elements in terms of rigorous research findings generated by an extensive array of highly credible scholars from various academic disciplines. Unlike the neoconservative ideologues who saturate our media with outlandish, baseless propaganda, I use the footnotes to establish some real-world accuracy and objectivity in the book, even if events in the fable are somewhat exaggerated in places. These footnotes explain how the symbolism in the story represents many aspects of the neoconservative excesses and narrow-mindedness in our currently right-wing-dominated, globalized world. In chapter 8, for example, if you want to know why the eminent, 18th-century Scottish economist Adam Smith crawls out of his grave to protest the abuse of the giant invisible hand of the marketplace, footnotes revealing the work of prominent economists and philosophers will clarify his reasons. A few examples among many scholarly analyses represented in the footnotes include critiques of neoconservative economic blunders by prominent economists such as John Kenneth Galbraith,

Paul Krugman, Robert Nadeau, and Ha-Joon Chang; portrayals of political and ideological dogmatism and corruption provided by political scientists Simone Chambers and Jacob Hacker and Paul Pierson; discussions of serious distortions and ethical problems in the media by philosopher Andrew Belsey and public policy researcher James Hamilton; and refutations of historical distortions provided by historian Joan W. Scott.

Finally, here's a preview of your trip. Throughout this volume you will follow the journey of Seymour Prober, an investigative journalist from a foreign nation, and his guide, Parochial Spinner, a representative of the Neoconian Propaganda Ministry, as they visit important people and places throughout the nation. First, you'll experience the last few nautical miles of Seymour's voyage across the Great Sea into the port of Daft Harbor and then on into the capital city of Fascisto. Here you will come to understand the Neoconian system of government while meeting prominent politicians and a charismatic televangelist. Parochial Spinner will explain the workings of the government agencies as well as the Lobbyists who really pull the strings in the capital. You'll see the Golden Slab, an artifact that controls the minds of all Neoconians as if by magic. Along the way, you'll gain a peek into the operations of the Weasel News television network, which fuels the zealotry of all citizens while striking fear into the hearts of anyone who dares to disagree. Later, you'll meet the fishmen fellows who swim in the think-tank waters and provide the shallow, murky intellectual justification for the Neoconian system. In the interior of the nation, you'll flee from Adam Smith's invisible hand as it curls into an iron fist while the people of Atomistia play the game of Marketopia in Selfish Valley. You'll also visit with Adam Smith himself as he complains about current abuses of his invisible hand. Later on you'll go shopping in Big Boxica, a hedonistic, egomaniacal, materialist's paradise. Your next stops will be White City and Toxica along the banks of Flaming Filth River in Empathy Gulf Valley. While there, you'll see the impressive factories that make up the industrial core of the nation. You'll also perceive contrasts such as starving children picking through garbage on Trash Mountain only a few miles from the ostentatious estate of a blue-blooded aristocrat of enormous wealth and minimal brain. As Seymour and Parochial begin the last leg of their trip you'll come to appreciate the cutting-edge scientific research that grossly inflates the busts of upper-class Neoconian women while making well-heeled, old Neoconian men the most efficient geriatric erectors in the world. The innovative schools that force-feed compliance juice to the children also should capture your attention if not your admiration. Speaking of compliance, your last few stops will take you to the largest and most efficient prison complex known to humankind where executions are fun and organs are harvested, and finally to the enormous military base just as the

Don Ambrose

Neoconians launch yet another massive invasion of a foreign land to rid it of
evildoers in the name of national glory.

As with any trip to a foreign land, it is wise for you to know a little
about the place in advance so you'll be able to navigate everyday challenges
and appreciate the culture. Here are some things you need to know about
Neoconland before making your imaginary visit to the island:

1. Most featured characters are male because testosterone and
    patriarchal tradition dominate the culture and ideology of
    the nation. While the Neoconians make some noise about
    equal rights for women, one of their important goals is to
    protect and strengthen male dominance in the culture.
2. Race is not much of an issue in the nation because virtually
    all Neoconians are white and Eurocentric. Aside from a few
    token minority ideologues who carefully toe the party line,
    it's hard to tell whether or not there are any other races or
    ethnicities represented in the population, and if there are
    others, where they went and why.
3. The nation seems quite harmonious because citizens typically
    don't raise difficult questions or contemplate the nuances of
    complex issues. Anyone who does is attacked as a muddle-
    headed fool, a flip-flopper, or a _____ lover (fill in the blank
    with the name of any despised enemy).

It's time for you to start your adventure. I hope you enjoy tagging along
with Seymour Prober as he visits with a wide variety of peculiar, ignorant,
dangerous, and corrupt neocons in their cities, factories, schools, prisons, and
military bases. Take your antidepressant, buckle your seatbelt, and check your
moral compass. It's going to be a wild ride.

─── CH 1. ───

SAILING INTO DAFT HARBOR

I'm Seymour Prober, senior investigative reporter from the Neutral Lands Gazette, *the leading newspaper in the Eastern Neutral Lands. This story recounts my troubling experiences during the most interesting and challenging assignment of my career. As the Gazette's leading reporter, I was assigned by my editors to do a story on the powerful island nation of Neoconland across the Great Sea. What follows includes transcriptions from the audio recordings I made during the trip as well as some brief narrations (in italics) to give you a sense of locations and events. I'm sure you'll agree that this great adventure took me into a nation like no other on earth.*

With a lurching stomach, I leaned over the deck railing of the Diehard Regressive, the passenger liner that was bringing me into the port town of Daft Harbor in the island nation of Neoconland. The passage across the Great Sea had been rough to say the least, generating frequent nausea and periodic vertigo. Even in late spring, tempests were brewing induced by global warming, which was disrupting the climate in disturbing ways. Overcoming my queasiness long enough to scan the harbor, I gained a panoramic view of a formerly idyllic cove rimmed with an expansive beach crowded by upscale resort hotels oddly interspersed with canneries and grimy coal-loading terminals. As the boat nudged up to the wharf, floating dead fish, detergent froth, and murky, gray water shattered my expectations of crystal-clear aquamarine shallows. But I wasn't here on vacation. As an investigative journalist from the 2000-mile distant Neutral Lands, I was on a mission to discover the truth about this vibrant, powerful nation of Neoconland, which had become so influential in commerce and military affairs internationally. While disembarking, I looked for my government-appointed guide, Parochial Spinner, a gregarious fellow assigned by the National Propaganda Ministry of the Neoconian government to accompany me throughout my long trip. As I wrestled my bags down the gangway a bearish voice called out:

Spinner: Sir, you in the Bermuda shorts, Are you Mr. Prober, Mr. Seymour Prober of the Neutral Lands Gazette? I'm your guide Parochial Spinner from the National Propaganda Ministry. But just call me Spinner."[1]

Prober: Yes, good to meet you Mr. Spinner. I'm very much looking forward to the tour.

Spinner: Here, toss your bags into the back of my SUV. Sorry about the vehicle. They wanted me to tour you around in a much bigger EEM but we need a smaller vehicle to get into some of the places we'll be going.

Prober: Your SUV looks plenty big to me. It's three times the size of anything we drive in the Neutral Lands. What is an EEM anyway? And what's the National Propaganda Ministry?

Spinner: Let's hit the road. EEM means Excessive Egomobile, the biggest private vehicles on the planet. You'll be seeing a lot of them on our roads. And the National Propaganda Ministry assigns people like me to important visitors so they get to understand how perfect our utopian nation really is. Hey, let's stop at this resort hotel for a drink so you can settle your stomach and get your bearings.

We pulled into the parking lot of the most palatial hotel I've ever seen. A parking attendant rushed to take our keys while we stepped out onto a balcony overlooking the harbor. Seated at a table with a Tailspin Cocktail in my hand, I asked Spinner about the harbor and this hotel.

Spinner: Daft Harbor used to be a pristine resort until the industries started to move in. When the government deregulated everything the coal-loading terminals had just as much right to be here as the homes and resort hotels. In the early days this hotel was a world-famous resort, the best in the land. Then it changed hands and it turned into a prison for the rich and famous who were jailed for insider trading, tax evasion, violent union busting, and other crimes. Well, they were considered crimes in the old days before we Neoconians took over the government. Can you believe the silly things they used to do back then? During its prison years it housed a small handful of incarcerated corporate executives and socialites. Each of them had

---

1   Parochial Spinner got his name from the strong right-wing habit of employing propaganda and spinning news stories to put their narrow, parochial, ideological perspectives in the best possible light (for examples see Hacker & Pierson, 2005).

his or her own floor with a large personal staff: personal assistants, valets, chefs, maids, and the like. Shortly after the neocon revolution the wealthy were made virtually immune to criminal prosecution so this hotel reverted back to a resort again.

Peering over the balcony railing next to our table I marveled at the crystal clarity of the water and the abundance of beautiful tropical fish, which I certainly didn't see anywhere else in the polluted harbor. I asked Spinner why this pool of paradise existed beside such foul water.

Mechanical fish swimming in artificial lagoon adjacent to polluted Daft Harbor

Spinner: You can't see it but there's a glass-block wall barrier separating the water near the resort from the sea. It's really an engineering marvel because it creates the illusion of an invisible barrier between the clean and dirty water. The resort owners wanted the proper ambience for this outside bar so they created the artificial lagoon. And most of those tropical fish aren't real. There are a few live Tiger Barbs and Red Top Zebras in the lagoon but only a few because most fish in this part of the world are now extinct.[2] The ones in this lagoon are worth a lot of money. Most of the fish you see in here are mechanical. The manufacturer did a pretty good job with them because they look so real. But if you look closely you'll see the wind-up keys on their tops and the little propellers in their tails. Late at night you'll see workers swimming around in the lagoon winding up the keys of fish that stopped running and sank to the bottom. You know, some people still complain that pollution is ruining the harbor but they should stop their bellyaching. These artificial fish in this clear lagoon provide a great example of what a little entrepreneurial spirit can do.

We're a little late for our first stop so let's hop back in the SUV. Fortunately, we don't have far to go. The port town of Daft Harbor is just a few miles from Fascisto, the capital city where we'll take in some of the institutions that make this nation the greatest on earth. After that, we'll move on to other points of interest. I hope you're well rested because we have a lot to see and do.

---

2   Human economic activity is causing mass extinctions unparalleled since the disappearance of the dinosaurs (Wilson, 2002). The neoconservative love of unrestrained economic growth runs directly counter to the conservation initiatives required to solve this large-scale, global problem.

TOURING FASCISTO:
THE CAPITAL CITY

We drove slowly into the city so I wouldn't miss anything. My most striking observation about Fascisto was the stark difference between the developments on the left and right sides of the street we were driving along. The right side was crowded with new construction while the left was run down and nearly abandoned. Spinner said this town would change my thinking about politics forever because the capital city was where governance was being reinvented.

Spinner: We're heading up History Avenue, which is the main drag because it divides the city in two. There's been a lot of vigorous building on the right side of the avenue—many new industries, government buildings, and so on. The left side of the city has been in serious decay for several decades so you'll see a lot of cranes with wrecking balls over there. Kind of looks like a war zone. OK, as we go along here I'll just point out some of the important spots on both sides. See that lit-up complex with the neon signs? That's Weasel News, the main media outlet in the nation. You'll get a chance to see inside later. Have a look at its counterpart, National Community Media (NCM) on the left side of the street. Weasel News does a much better job of investigating and reporting because they're owned by our best tycoons and they hire the most skilled reporters. NCM on the other hand operates on a shoestring with only a few tired, old journalists who are ready for the retirement home. They even have to canvass their few listeners and viewers for donations if you can believe it. Nobody pays much attention to them anymore. All they do is interview a few of the crazy, old professors who used to work at the now defunct public universities. Who wants to listen to navel-gazing intellectuals when you can switch the channel to Weasel News and watch the video they shoot with hidden cameras in the bathrooms of the stars. How can you compete with Weasel's 24-7 coverage of the weeklong marriage-and-divorce, train-wreck relationship between the heiress and socialite Bimbo Jumbobazoom and the country music star Peahead Lummox? As you can see, there are some carpenters boarding up some of the windows on the broken-down, old NCM building.

Prober: Aren't the Weasel News shows you mentioned just entertainment, not news? I can't imagine them having any news value.

Spinner: I know you're a newsman in your country but aren't you going a bit far to substitute your judgment for that of the top executives at Weasel News? They're the leaders of the best media outlet in the nation so obviously they know what's news and what's not.

Prober: I just thought there must be more important things going on. Anyway, your news here may not be important but it is interesting. But what's happening on the sidewalks is even more fascinating. I notice that the pedestrians are stopping every few steps to put coins in boxes so a toll barrier will rise and let them proceed. What's going on here?

Spinner: Those are our toll sidewalks.[3] They started in the city of Big Boxica, our commercial and financial center, and then spread throughout the nation because the auto companies, led by Larceny Motors, and the oil-refining subsidiary of Coughing Coal-Black Industries, wanted people to drive more. They thought these toll sidewalks would encourage pedestrians to buy more cars and do more driving. First, they considered outlawing walking in public but that seemed a bit excessive. Fortunately, some fellows at the Glorious Birthright Foundation, one of our best think tanks, came up with the toll sidewalk idea and vehicle sales shot up about 20%. I tell you, those think-tank fellows are geniuses. Oh, have a look over here on the right again. Now we're passing Homicidal Industries, the nation's biggest gun manufacturer and distributor. It's that large building with the bulls-eye logo.

Prober: Why are so many school buses in their parking lot?

---

3   The neoconservative era has generated a frenzy of privatization through which public assets paid for by taxpayers over the course of decades are transferred to private hands, often at fire-sale prices and with little consideration of the ethical consequences (Phillips, 2002). Privatizing our infrastructure poses ethical problems because corporate loyalty is to the bottom line and not to the needs of the public.

Spinner: That must be their Guns for Kids Jamboree.[4] The Guns for Kids program is one of the most important charities in the land. The Federal Assault Rifle Confederacy, Homicidal Industries, and the Scrapburger fast-food chain joined forces to help make kids into better citizens. The kids save up their Scrapburger receipts. The more burgers they eat the sooner they qualify for prizes, which are guns of varying calibers and sizes depending on the number of receipts they have. Collecting 200 receipts gets them a small Derringer but 500 gets them a bolt-action .30-06 single-shot rifle. Big eaters saving 1000 receipts can get a .357 magnum revolver. And then there's the big prize. If they collect 2000 receipts they earn two monogrammed Boneshredder assault rifles complete with a year's supply of ammo plus a bonus pack of two-dozen fragmentation grenades. What kid can resist that? And the folks at Homicidal Industries are very generous. They bring the kids together at these jamborees once a month to give them marksmanship training. Last year they made the training more authentic when they bought some death-row prisoners from Wretched Warehouse Prison and set them loose in an open field for the kids to hunt down. Weasel News televised that jamboree in their kiddy-hour programming and it was a ratings hit.

Prober: Isn't that dangerous giving high-powered weapons to kids?

Spinner: Hey, guns don't kill people. Kids kill people. When we reach the point where every kid has a gun you can bet there won't be any more playground bullying! And when every teacher has a Boneshredder assault rifle there won't be any discipline problems in the schools. What's more, these kids will be more than ready to join the military when they graduate from school. In fact, some of our senators have approved the use of kiddy brigades in the army so they can participate in our frequent invasions of the Vassal Lands. That's good for the nation and great for the kids' character.

Prober: What are the Vassal Lands?

Spinner: That's our name for the foreign countries overseas. We call them all Vassal Lands because many of them belong to us, even if they don't know it yet. Our corporations own most of their resources and we acquire more every time we invade them.[5]

Crack! A bullet hole appeared in my passenger-side window.

---

4 America has by far the highest rate of shooting homicides and suicides among the developed nations. Our children have far too easy access to firearms (see Edlin & Golanty, 2006).

5 Prominent scholars worry that the corporate, financial, and media forces of globalization may represent the most visible components of a new form of imperialism (Howe, 2002).

Prize winner at Guns for Kids Jamboree

Prober: Would you mind if we move on—quickly?! I'm anxious to see what's up the street.

Spinner: Oh yeah, sure. I knew this town would get you excited. I mentioned Wretched Warehouse Prison a minute ago. It's over those hills to the northeast not far from the city. We'll head there later in the trip. Look out to our left at that old, gray building on Distributive Justice Street. That's called Worker Union Hall. Not much left of it is there?[6] The guys with the wrecking ball have most of it down. Want to watch the last of it fall?

───────────────

6   Several decades of economic restructuring, largely along the lines of neoconservative ideology, have eroded union influence and membership

Prober: Not really. Look just ahead of us on both sides of the road. They're even knocking down some churches, synagogues, and a mosque with wrecking balls. Why are they doing that?

Spinner: Frankly, we don't need them anymore since we unified all of our old religions to create the Maniacal Cult of Intolerant Absolutism, or the MCIA. Now all people in the land follow the word of Intolerant Absolutism and they meet several times a week in our megachurches like that one over there on the right side of the Avenue.[7]

Prober: Wow! That's enormous! It looks like a very large, domed football stadium.

Spinner: It holds about 200,000 followers, so it does have far more capacity than any of our sports stadiums. But there's a more important story here. Aside from its obvious worth to our individual citizens, the Maniacal Cult of Intolerant Absolutism may have been the catalyst for our transformation from the old, inefficient, corrupt society we barely tolerated in the past to our new utopia. It mobilized the citizens to become activists who supported our leaders without question, thereby enabling them to tear down all those useless old buildings in FDR Plaza, for example. It also gave us stronger motivation to invade the heathen Vassal Lands.

Prober: How did the MCIA mobilize its followers so well?

Spinner: It took a leader of truly gargantuan proportions and massive charisma. Fortunately, a man by the name of Abominate Frenzy, or "Loving Abe" as we fondly call him now, became our messianic leader. His fire-and brimstone, apocalyptic sermons terrified the masses while hardening their resolve to remake the world in his image. The first thing they did was to tear down the old religious symbols and replace them with Loving Abe's picture. Notice that even the old houses of worship they're tearing down no longer have the Christian Cross, the Star of David, the Star and Crescent, or any other symbol of reverence. Look again at the top of the megachurch. You'll see Abominate Frenzy's 50-foot-high smiling image prominently erected over each of the four sides of the building. It's even more impressive at night because they light up his face with airport searchlights. After they tore down the old religious symbols, they rounded up all the priests, ministers, rabbis, and mullahs and exiled them to the Vassal Lands. So now Abominate Frenzy is the one and only true voice. But maybe I should say he's the primary voice

---

(Fairbrother & Griffin, 2002). Consequently, the needs and views of workers lack representation in the global socioeconomic arena.

7 Cult leaders like Abominate Frenzy gain much of their influence by convincing people that the nation is in moral decline, having rejected important values. But the idea that America is suffering erosion of values in a culture war is overblown (Baker, 2005).

of the one true word, because there are other leaders doing similar work, although they're not nearly as messianic.[8]

Abominate Frenzy

8   Abominate Frenzy enjoyed another significant advantage. He rose to power because extremist fundamentalism emerges and strengthens in a society when people feel threatened economically, politically, or socially. In such conditions, they crave secure, stable, and unquestioned group identities, and fundamentalism provides these certainties (Marty & Appleby, 1994). The harsh, exploitative economic conditions of Neoconland generate sufficient economic and social threat to drive millions into Abominate Frenzy's flock. His fire and brimstone sermons generate the illusion of additional threat and uncertainty, thereby bringing him even more recruits. According to Bohm (1994) and Campbell (1993), religions tend to have very positive, uplifting core values in common such as compassion, tolerance, and altruism. But these more reasonable, nuanced messages of mainstream religions cannot compete with the Maniacal Cult of Intolerant Absolutism (MCIA), because they lack the morbid fascination of Abominate Frenzy's apocalyptic storytelling coupled with the psychological soother of absolute certainty provided by the MCIA. Moore (2000) revealed the dark side of feverish religious movements, showing how mass moral beliefs can lead to vicious persecutions. Influential religious authorities such as Abominate Frenzy often portray outsiders or "nonbelievers" as impure polluters whose very existence represents intolerable moral failure and violations of God's will. As a result, devout followers find it easy to engage in discrimination and even violent attacks against outsiders. These dynamics underpinned many of the most reprehensible acts of mass violence in human history (Moore; Stark, 2003).

Prober: What will happen when he passes away?

Spinner: Most people don't think he will die because he'll be resurrected again and again. But if he does leave us we'll be fine because his son, Howler Frenzy, is being groomed to take Abominate's place. Howler is a chip off the old block. He has the same stature, demeanor, well-oiled hairstyle, even the same booming voice. I don't think the MCIA would skip a beat if Abominate left us, as sad as that would be.

Prober: What are those bunker-like structures on the right just past the megachurch? See those stainless steel and concrete bunkers bristling with periscopes and satellite dishes?

Spinner: Cool, aren't they? Those are our secret police headquarters. Notice they don't really stand out except for the big, fluorescent, red-and-white "TOP-SECRET" signs, because they're so secret. But I'm a member of the Savage Swine—a super-super-secret, highly exclusive Dogma University society so I'm an insider and I can tell you what some of our secret police organizations are, at least some of them. Nobody knows all of them. We'll stop by these bunkers for a minute so I can tell you more about them.

Citizen Monitoring Bureau Secret Police and Spy Bunker

Prober: Please do. I'm very interested.

Spinner: This first bunker labeled "Top Secret" is the headquarters of the Citizen Monitoring Bureau, or the CMB. As you likely guessed, they carefully watch every citizen in the country, except for a few at the top. They try to ensure that everyone follows the directives of the Golden Slab, the historical document you'll see at our next stop. The cool thing about the CMB is the way they keep bad people in line. They have so many domestic agents watching us that nobody with deviant thoughts can expect to do an evil deed and get away with it.

Prober: Don't your citizens see anything wrong with domestic spying? I heard your nation was founded on freedom. So much intrusive spying seems like a violation of human rights.

Savage Swine Secret
Society Member

Spinner: Don't be silly. These agents are domestic overseers, not spies. And they are carefully selected by our leaders who ensure that all of our agents are morally correct. Thanks to the CMB, disgusting people like feminists, gays, progressives, environmentalists, intellectuals, and peace activists either reform or they're driven deep underground. The next bunker, the one with the "Top-Top Secret" sign, houses the Reprobate Intelligence Agency, which spies on all the Vassal Lands to select those most promising for overthrow or invasion.[9] The RIA finds out which foreign nations have the most resources and the weakest military forces so the corporation that owns our military, Apocalypse Industries, can maximize their profits of conquest while minimizing losses. Without the help of the RIA our imperial empire wouldn't be nearly as large today. The third bunker with the "Unbelievably Hush Hush Super Secret"

---

9 Our secret agencies have a long track record of interfering in the affairs of other nations even to the point of catalyzing the overthrow of democratic governments and supporting the installation of despotic regimes more aligned with our corporate interests. Our support of the reprehensible Pinochet regime in Chile (see Klein, 2008; Kornbluh, 2003) and the Shah of Iran (see Kinzer, 2006) are two of many examples. Neocons have moral blind spots when it comes to the heinous nature of their dictator friends. Former British Prime Minister Margaret Thatcher, for example, continued to laud Pinochet as a hero long after the atrocities of his regime became common knowledge (Ensalaco, 2005). See the discussion of Apocalypse Industries and Wartown in Chapter 15 for elaboration.

sign is the Bestial Shadow Agency, which spies on the first two secret-police organizations to make sure they act in the best interests of the Emperor, our head of government, because he has to have firm control over the nation to be an effective despot. Unfortunately, that's the limit of my knowledge about these places. The other 13 bunkers you see keep us safe and moral by doing other things about which we can only guess. By the way, don't ask me any more questions about these secret-police agencies because foreigners aren't supposed to know about them.

Prober: All right, but I have a different question. You mentioned a Savage Swine secret society. How do you join it and what's it for?[10]

Spinner: It's an exclusive club at Dogma University. You don't just get in! You have to be from one of the best families and you must have a proven track record of correct belief, correct behavior, and substantial inheritance. If that gets you in, you have to dress up in Druid costumes and pig noses at night and urinate on one another while chanting some ancient phrases that nobody understands. The pig snouts are real. They're imported from the slaughterhouses in our industrial town of Toxica, and we use duct tape to attach them to our faces for the meetings. Most Savage Swine meetings wrap up with blood-drinking sacrifices starting with a few pigs from the big factory farms and ending with several lower-class people known as Putrid Scum, who are brought in from Homeless Alley or the prison. Darn it! I'm not supposed to tell anybody about what we do at our meetings. You won't report this, will you?

Prober: If I do, it will be in a foreign land.

Spinner: That's a relief! Foreign lands don't count and Weasel News doesn't do any foreign reporting unless we're invading someone. We should move on. Look to your left once again. There's FDR Plaza, the biggest complex on the wrong side of History Avenue. The plaza used to be the hotbed of wrong thinking where all the muddleheaded liberals, or "progressives," came from. As you can see, the wrecking ball has demolished much of it. That pile of rubbish over there used to be the Universal Health Care Hospital. They never finished building it and now it's just a pile of broken concrete, as it should be. Did you know that in the old days, before the neocons took over the nation, the government had the audacity to tax us high-class Bluebloods and use the money in attempts to build that ridiculous hospital so the low-class Near Dregs and Putrid Scum could have quality medical care? What a waste! Now look a little further down the plaza at the Civil Rights Building

---

10 Resurgences of conservatism in our culture are accompanied by a particular set of beliefs and behaviors including the emergence of secret societies complete with passwords, secret handshakes, and arcane rituals (Aho, 2006).

on Affirmative Action Boulevard. The progressives thought they had finished constructing that building but the wreckers are busy tearing it down.[11] There won't be much left of it in a month or so. These and all the other buildings are coming down to make room for another Box Kingdom Supermall like the one in Big Boxica. They're also putting in a new Revisionist History Museum where what's left of the Civil Rights building stands. The museum will tell the true story of our history based on the correct thinking of our best political leaders. We can't wait for this side of Fascisto to complete its urban renewal.

Prober: I see a very interesting building back over on the right side of History Avenue. Can we take a closer look?

Spinner: Of course. No tour of Fascisto would be complete without a look at the Zealots' Court Building, where the laws of the land are interpreted and enforced. This is an important pillar of our plutocracy. Nine of our top judges are appointed to the Zealots' Court to make sure our laws are correct.

Prober: You said plutocracy. Don't you mean democracy?[12]

Spinner: No, no. We tried democracy for a while back in the dark, old days, but it soon became evident that only the right people could run this nation well, and they all come from Blueblood stock. With the government in the hands of a few super-wealthy individuals, it frees everyone else to go about their business of self-infatuation.

Prober: Very interesting! Back to the Zealots' Court. Who appoints the judges?

Spinner: Actually, that's still a very democratic process. They're appointed by our top leaders including the Emperor, Abominate Frenzy of the Maniacal Cult of Intolerant Absolutism, and the CEOs of our six largest corporations. Abominate Frenzy and each of the CEOs controls his own judge and the Emperor controls two. So, each judge represents the interests of his

---

11 Strong criticism of government bureaucracy as inefficient has been forcing governments to trim both the size and effectiveness of their departments. This trend is undermining the strength and survival of democracy, which relies on healthy bureaucracies for its maintenance (Suleiman, 2003).

12 The presence of democracy in a nation does not automatically make that nation fair, just, and benevolent. According to Wolfe (2006), influential right-wing individuals and groups in America have made themselves the beneficiaries of government policies by enacting corrupt initiatives such as deregulation of environmental protection and the implementation of immoral tax policies that shift the burden away from the affluent toward the middle class. Neoconservative ideology has pushed us away from democratic governance toward a plutocratic system, which entails rule by the privileged few (Ambrose, 2005; Webb & Webb, 1995; Wolin, 2008).

constituency.[13] There's a judge for Coughing Coal-Black Industries, one for Stupor Drugs, another for Homicidal Industries, another for the Scrapburger fast-food chain, and so on. As with most of our institutions, the Zealots' Court is a model for the rest of the world. They've made some very important legal decisions lately. For example, in the case of Recalcitrant vs. Frenzy, they ruled that Abominate Frenzy had the right to impose compulsory tri-weekly church attendance as a requirement of employment anywhere in the nation. In another case, NCEA vs. Lobbyville, they protected the free speech of lobbyists in Fascisto by ruling that there should be no restrictions on their freedom to buy politicians' votes in the legislature. They rapped the knuckles of the Neoconland Civil Ethics Association on that one. I can't believe the NCEA still exists! They lose every time they try to implement one of their crackpot schemes. They should learn sooner or later.

Prober: How can the court call manipulating the legislative process through buying votes free speech? Sounds more like corruption to me.

Spinner: Oh, you're way off base there! The lobbyists obviously have to speak to the politicians to set up the backroom financial deals, so obviously it's a free-speech issue. What would you have them do? Use smoke signals? The judges on the Zealots' court are the finest legal minds in the nation so obviously their decisions are right. Oh, we're running short of time and there are a few more places we have to visit in Fascisto. Let's drive on.

At the far south end of the city we approached a formidable brick wall completely blocking History Avenue. There were a number of large, marble statues on top of the wall, all standing in heroic postures with right arms outstretched pointing back toward the center of Fascisto. Neoconland flags fluttered from poles located between the statues along the wall.

Prober: Very impressive! Please tell me about this monument.

Spinner: Yes it is impressive indeed. This is the End of History Wall built to commemorate the founding of our utopia.[14] It's become somewhat of a

---

13 The Supreme Court allowed the bias of its members to influence one of its most important decisions in history, effectively appointing the Bush-Cheney ticket to the presidency in spite of the harmful precedent it set (Dershowitz, 2002). While the popular media reinforces the notion that liberal ideologues promote dangerous judicial activism to promote near-socialist causes, the opposite is closer to the truth. For the past three decades, our higher courts have been marching inexorably rightward and engaging in ever-more extreme right-wing judicial activism in attempts to dismantle protective legal regulations (Sunstein, 2005).

14 Fukuyama (1992) famously claimed that liberal democracies built upon neoclassical economic systems represent the "end of history" and the apex of sociopolitical and economic evolution. Scott (2001) argued that Fukuyama's assumptions about the end of history represent an interesting case of referential

shrine and every citizen of Neoconland wants to visit it at least once in a lifetime. It was inspired by a book titled *History: Done Like Dinner* written by Hidebound Flimflam III Esquire, a prominent fellow from the Neoconland Chicanery Institute think tank. His book proved beyond the shadow of a doubt that the ascendance of our first Emperor and the emergence of the Golden Slab represented the climax of history and that Neoconland represented the highest form of human development. This wall at the end of History Avenue symbolizes just that—the end of history.

Prober: What's beyond the wall?

Spinner: Nobody knows anymore because there's no reason to look past it. See the statues of past Emperors and prominent corporate leaders on the wall. They all point back at the past, not forward. They remind us to follow our traditions without question. They remind us that father knows best, greed is good, our beliefs are good and all others are evil, things like that. We should drive along the coast just out of the city so you can visit the Golden Slab, the greatest document in the history of humanity.

---

illusion based on the artificial sanitization of history. The illusion comes from assumptions that the reports of historians were objective and truthful when, in reality, they were saturated with the historians' own subjective impressions and ideological biases. In short, historians are bound up in the culture and ideology of their times so they must be keenly aware of their own biases if they want to be accurate. Fukuyama regularly travels in neoconservative circles so the onus is on him to guard against utopian, neoconservative interpretations of history. McMurtry (2002) illustrated some flaws in the thinking of those who proclaimed the admirable victory of neoconservative/neoliberal ideology and free-market economics, which manifests as relentless socioeconomic globalization. After illustrating the devastating effects of neoliberal globalization—which include excessive privatization and deregulation of public institutions and services, severe ecological damage, and sociopolitical turmoil—he concluded that the current globalized system cannot prevail over the long term because it is based on inhuman values. In an earlier work, McMurtry (1999) used the term "cancer stage of capitalism" to characterize these phenomena because there are profound and disturbing parallels between neoliberal globalization of the world and the characteristics of a cancerous attack on the human body. Along similar lines, Woodward and Simms (2006) showed how globalization is hurting the world's poor by reducing their already paltry share of the world's resources while burdening them with the harmful side effects of development. Heilbroner (1994) argued that capitalism must be guided and controlled to some extent if it is to generate more benefit than harm.

Сн 3.

The Golden Slab

Caught in rush-hour traffic, even though it wasn't rush hour, I was relieved when we turned off into the parking lot of the Golden Slab Museum, which perched majestically on a cliff overlooking the Great Sea. We walked into the building and, with the help of Spinner's government VIP pass, avoided the long line of pilgrims who were waiting patiently for their view of an artifact that meant so much to them. With apparent relish, Spinner launched into an obviously well-worn speech about the solid chunk of rock on the dais before us.

Spinner: This just could be the high point of your entire trip! Here, you get to see the Golden Slab, the discovery that guided us out of a wimpy, liberal past into our glorious present. You've heard of important documents and artifacts like the Magna Carta, the Rosetta Stone, and the American Declaration of Independence. Well the Golden Slab has them all beat.

Prober: I heard something about the slab on the boat trip here. Please tell me more.

Spinner: We used to have a constitution that laid out citizens' rights and responsibilities as well as the separation of powers in the various branches of government. But we found it too cumbersome. It kept getting in the way when our Emperor or our lobbyists wanted to accomplish something, so we tore it up gradually, clause by clause so the radical liberal mushies wouldn't get too whiny, and then our greatest think-tank minds met in secret one afternoon

17

to replace it.[15] At the conclusion of their meeting, one of their leaders by the name of Faux Oracle went up Mt. Exclusion, our tallest mountain, for a few days and then came down with the Golden Slab in a wheelbarrow. Nobody knows how he found it but it was a major discovery: a shining moment in our history.[16] The slab is a translucent, almost transparent quartz-like stone with a golden hue. You normally see quartz in crystal form, but the slab is flat and smooth. And the most amazing thing about it is the inscription. It has 10 directives or rules of life carved into its face and Faux Oracle said they were there when he found it. Now the 10 directives of the slab are taught every day in every grade level in every school. They hang over the doorway of every courthouse and municipal building in the land. Here, I'll close my eyes and recite the directives to you.

1. With thine own self be infatuated obsessively!
2. Exalt self-reliance!
3. Economic fundamentalism forever!
4. Honor private property above all else!
5. Privatize public assets!
6. Greed is good!
7. Dogma forever!
8. More! More! Bigger! Bigger! At all costs![17]

---

15 The Bush administration aggressively chipped away at civil liberties and magnified the power of the executive branch of government in the name of national security (Mille, 2004; Wolin, 2008).

16 The Golden Slab signifies a utopian vision of neoconservative politics as a form of religion. According to Gentile (2006) the political aspect of a nation becomes "religious" when the political system comes to be viewed as sacred based on "an unchallengeable monopoly of power, ideological monism, and the obligatory and unconditional subordination of the individual and collectivity to its code of commandments. Consequently, a political religion is intolerant, invasive, and fundamentalist" (p. xv).

17 Economic growth is a seldom-questioned goal of neoconservative ideology and neoclassical economic theory, which is a cornerstone of neoconservatism. However, the results of unchecked growth include the degradation, depletion, and unequal distribution of resources around the world. These resource issues are pushing us toward serious social disruptions such as ethnic disputes, urban unrest, insurrections, mass migrations, and the aggravation of already severe poverty (Homer-Dixon, 2001). Free-trade systems put in place by neoclassical economics and neoconservative ideologues have generated stark inequality, the erosion of workers' rights, and dangerous economic instability in many parts of the world (Saul, 2005). "Overconsumptive" economics presents us with a huge ethical challenge (Mayer, 1998; Westra & Werhane, 1998). Nadeau

9. Be wary of the foreign![18]
10. Protect family values!

Prober: It's impressive that you knew them so well and could recite them, so fluently.

The Golden Slab

Spinner: Well, I did go to the best school in the land and we practiced slab recitation every day.

(2003) recommended the replacement of neoclassical economics with a new, environmentally responsible form of economic theory and research.

18 The Nazis engaged in horrific acts partly because they had a powerful sense of right and wrong based on their sense of righteousness about their ethnic superiority and their loathing of outsiders (Weitz, 2003).

Prober: Actually seeing the slab is quite an honor. May I have a closer look?

Spinner: Yes, but be very careful! The guards can get quite antsy.

The slab certainly was weighty, at least in terms of weight. Noticing the light from a desk lamp gleaming through a corner of the slab, I crawled under the glass dais and right under the slab itself to see if the sunshine from the skylight at the top of the museum would show through. To my astonishment, the sunlight revealed some deeply embedded writing on the hidden bottom of the slab. From my position directly under the center of the slab, this previously obscured writing appeared in parentheses after each commandment. In ordinary light, these words were invisible; however, exposed to the light of day from just the right angle the slab became more transparent and its hidden meaning shone through. Here again is the text from the slab showing its hidden meanings in italics:

1. With thine own self be infatuated obsessively! *and completely ignore the needs and rights of others!*
2. Exalt self-reliance! *but support thine offspring and cronies with nepotism and kickbacks!*
3. Economic fundamentalism forever! *while sacrificing ethics, altruism, and basic human necessities!*
4. Honor private property above all else! *and dismantle public goods like libraries, health care for all children, care for the elderly…!*[19]
5. Privatize public assets! *to enrich ourselves and our cronies at the expense of others!*[20]
6. Greed is good! *for shattering our souls!*

---

19 According to comparisons of gross domestic product (GDP), America is the most affluent nation in the world; however, measures of GDP ignore gross inequalities *within* nations. Studies that dig deeper into the nature of resources available for child development reveal that our levels of child poverty approach the worst among developed nations (Smeeding, Rainwater, & Burtless, 2002). Countries with somewhat less reverence for individualism and private property use government spending to alleviate child poverty thereby providing better life chances for all children.

20 Contrary to neoconservative belief, private enterprise does not do everything better than government (Galbraith, 1996; Kuttner, 1999). The free market has done a poor job with many aspects of medicine, finance, education, communications, and other sectors. Our medical care system is a prominent example. While providing excellent care for some, the largely privatized American medical system is the most costly in the world but rates poorly against other developed nations, many of which allocate strong influence to government agencies (Lasser, Himmelstein, & Woolhandler, 2006).

7. Dogma forever! *because closed minds avoid the pain of complex, nuanced thought!*
8. More! More! Bigger! Bigger! At all costs! *and who cares if my big toys ruin the environment? I'll be gone by then!*
9. Be wary of the foreign! *so we won't have to reconsider our own thoughts and ways!*
10. Protect family values! *while destroying millions of families worldwide!*

Excited, I almost shouted out my discovery but caught myself just in time. Looking around the Rotunda at the pious pilgrims, armed guards, and politicians, and keenly aware of their reverence for the slab, I realized this would not be a receptive audience.[21] *Waiting for a better time and place would be prudent. Instead, I planted a small mind seed.*

Prober: Has anyone looked closely at the Golden Slab? Have they inspected it with magnifying glasses or microscopes?

Spinner: Whatever for? Why would we want anyone messing around with our most treasured historical document? I think you should crawl out from beneath it now. You're making the guards jumpy and I don't fancy explaining

---

21 Neoclassical economics has been promoted vigorously as a highly successful, objective science that proves the validity of rules 1 through 6 and 8 of the Golden Slab. Nevertheless, a group of prominent economists recently revealed a considerable array of serious neoclassical flaws (see Fullbrook, 2004). Among the flaws are its (a) abuse of statistical analyses, (b) ignorance of major globalization issues, (c) inattention to environmental problems, and (d) lack of objectivity, which shows up in the strong tendency for influential neoclassical economists to narrow the economics curriculum in colleges while blocking the employment of economists who dissent from their dogma. Dissenting economists seem to be especially perturbed by the neoclassical penchant for elevating ideology above science. An academic journal, the *Post-Autistic Economics Review,* captures the essence of these complaints. The hubris of neoclassical economists shows up in their attempts to dominate the world's socioeconomic systems. Chang (2002) described the troubling consequences of neoclassical ideology taken too far, showing how developed nations force third-world nations to follow excessive free-market policies of extreme privatization and deregulation to their detriment by embedding these policies in the rules for economic-development loans. Ironically, the third-world economic growth ensuing from these rules is anemic, falling behind the growth patterns that prevailed before imposition of the neoclassical rules. Moreover, the neoclassically dominated developed nations themselves did not follow neoclassical rules when they were emerging from third-world status. Mexico provides a specific, infamous example, with its government now dominated by privatizing, budget-slashing, deregulating neoclassical economists (Babb, 2001).

to my superiors why you landed in prison in the first few hours of your stay here. Look at the time! We have to go anyway. We have an appointment at Weasel News studios, so fasten your seat belt.

CH 4.

RAT-LIKE GASBAGS AT
WEASEL NEWS

Spinner: Here we are at Weasel News, the state of the art for 21st-century objective, investigative journalism. Their motto is "If we don't report it, it doesn't exist." Let's go in and see the operation.

The Weasel News headquarters and studios were marvels of marketing. Large video screens constantly ran promo clips of feature news shows and documentaries. When shows were running, the ever-present text banners scrolled from right to left at the bottom of the screen displaying patriotic slogans and product advertisements.[22]

---

22 The civil society of a nation is unhealthy to the extent that its media is colonized and manipulated by money or power (Chambers, 2002). Postman (1985) warned some time ago that the images of television promote superficial glitz over substance. Consistent with his warnings, Belsey (1998) discerned troubling patterns in the evolution of journalism. Ethical, objective, investigative journalism is transforming into profit-centered, entertainment-driven journalism lacking in ethics. Hamilton (2003) described a similar shift from hard news about political issues to soft news about entertainment. The transition from ethical, hard news to entertaining news often entails the replacement of expensive but highly informative objective field reporting with inexpensive and morbidly entertaining but hollow arguments between venom-spewing, polarized pundits. Shallow, profit-driven reporting is a serious danger to our democracy, which requires the objective information and transparency provided by ethical investigation. Weasel

One of these said, "Want to show the secret police your patriotism? Buy your boy a Boneshredder assault rifle!" Another declared, "All of our emperors smoked Canker Cigarettes! Light up a Canker today." The Neoconland flag rippled majestically in the background of every scene. Large posters decorated the hallways and studio walls. Stopping to peruse one poster, I noticed that it illustrated a diabolical character in academic robes with blood dripping from its fangs and claws. A notation in the corner of the image said it was derived from the book The 35 Worst, Evil, Demonic, Wacko Professors. *Other posters either extolled the angelic and heroic virtues of corporate leaders, lobbyists, politicians, and military generals or attacked a variety of scientists, intellectuals, environmentalists, and various other politicians.*

Spinner: Here inside these acclaimed studios are some of our most famous, objective journalists in action. You're in for a special treat. I pulled

---

News takes superficiality to the extreme. A specific example of this problem comes from coverage of political issues and events. Today's media fails to analyze political campaigns with much depth and clarity, thus leaving the public with insufficient understanding of candidates and issues (Gans, 2003; Jamieson & Waldman, 2002; Shanor, 2003). Unfortunately, increasing concentration of the media in private, corporate hands (McChesney, 1999) manipulates public policy, and the individual citizen is dwarfed by powerful special interests. Adding insult to injury, the corporate owners of major media outlets have been lobbying to replace government regulation of their operations with voluntary self-regulation (Franklin & Pilling, 1998). All of this weakens our democracy, which depends on an informed citizenry. Too often the media's major product now is publicity for the president and other politicians, who should be subject to critique, not mindless cheerleading (Gans). For example, the mainstream media parroted the administration's claims about Iraq as an imminent menace in the run up to the war but ignored considerable evidence showing that these claims were fraudulent (Lance, Lawrence, & Livingston, 2007). The danger is clear because fascism relies on misinformation, deception, and propaganda to perpetuate itself (Passmore, 2002). Similar concerns arise from the work of the eminent philosopher Hannah Arendt, who decried deception and propaganda as caustic elements employed by those bent on dominating others in a society (see Presby, 1997). Patriotism has its place, and pride in one's nation or ethnicity plays an important part in personal identity formation. Nevertheless, excessive patriotism and group pride becomes dangerous because it can work up ordinary people into irrational frenzies, making them capable of great injustice and brutality (Kateb, 2006). It promotes particularist morality (good us vs. evil them) while suppressing universalist morality (a sense of unity with all of humanity). Particularism inclines us to help those most like ourselves while ignoring outsiders or even doing them violence (Gewirth, 1988). Universalist morality is characteristic of the highest forms of self-fulfillment while particularist morality allows only limited, somewhat hollow forms of self-fulfillment (Gewirth).

some strings and got us tickets putting us in the studio audience for the top-rated, highest-quality news program on the air today—the Pundit O. Gasbag show. As usual, he's interviewing some important people. These are his guests for today—Wimpy Sham Radical, a rather unsavory character, and Shrilly Noxious. Shrilly is the best-known reporter and expert commentator in the network. She made her name by cleverly telling stories about a whole host of foolish crimes that the liberal mushies might have committed. She's a great example of the Neoconian Dream because she came up from nothing. Weasel News executives found her wandering the streets after the residents of all the government insane asylums were released during the Great Privatization.[23]

Shrilly Noxious

---

23 President Reagan slashed budgets for mental health institutions and forced large numbers of mentally ill patients out onto the streets (Wisely, 2003).

After they trained her to be a reporter and commentator, she spent a lot of time in Fascisto looking across the street at FDR Plaza imagining the subversive rantings and depraved actions of muddle-headed mushies like Noble Compassion and her disgusting friend Livid Fairplay. She wrote news stories based on her imaginings and they were wonderful. Of course, she has her own large, piped-in supply of idea fuel from the ideological think-tank pipelines. I'll tell you more about the idea fuel later. Everyone is grateful to her for attacking those progressives. Noble Compassion is a noodle-brained idiot who's always pushing some useless, wasteful scheme for the betterment of children. She tries to get the government to pay for early childcare, orphanages for street children, and other silly things like that. Her friend Livid Fairplay is even worse. She constantly criticizes our honorable corporations and politicians, saying they abuse ordinary people through various acts of corruption. How does she come up with those crackpot ideas? Obviously, she's insane.

Prober: When Shrilly wrote her stories, didn't she go into FDR Plaza to fact check; you know, to see if her imaginings of these crimes were accurate?

Spinner: Come on now, you saw FDR Plaza from the street. It's such a dingy, despicable place that you just know what goes on there by looking from a distance. Besides, if our investigative reporters wasted their time fact checking, Weasel News would have to hire more of them and then the executives wouldn't be able to pay Pundit O. Gasbag enough to keep him happy. And the profits of the shareholders of the network would drop off.

Pundit O. Gasbag emerged from the dressing rooms to thunderous applause from the studio audience and kibitzed with some groupies while waiting for the show to start.

Prober: Pundit sure has a large mouth, and he's very loud!

Spinner: The Weasel News owners and executives looked far and wide for the best news anchor and talk-show host possible. They wanted someone predictable and convincing, someone who could get the message across assertively and with pizzazz. When they interviewed and auditioned the leading contenders they noticed something. They all had large, powerful lungs and mouths. The best of them could be heard throughout several city blocks without a megaphone. Of course, such large, bellowing mouths come with a sacrifice. Nature makes only so much room in the design of a person's head so an enormous mouth comes at the expense of the cranium, and this leaves room for only a very small brain. But the top brass at Weasel News were OK with that. They write the talking points for each show in simplistic, black-and-white terms and all the anchors and talk-show hosts have to do is recite them. Why complicate matters? And if guests use foul, devious lies to get the better of them in an argument, all they have to do is yell at them to shut up and then cut off their microphones. As long as the anchors can read at a fourth-grade level, recite, and yell they're fine because there's no need to think. They're heroic people of action, not useless, navel-gazing intellectuals. Pundit O. Gasbag is the best of them and the obvious choice, as you can see from his exceptionally large mouth and tiny cranium. Oh, watch! The show is starting.

Pundit O. Gasbag: Well Mr. Radical, some people say that you and your mushy, progressive friends have been unfairly criticizing our Emperor for making his brilliant, far-sighted, compassionate tax cuts on the wealthy Splendiferous Bluebloods while raising taxes on the no-good, working-class Near Dregs and using that money to build more prisons to house the low-life, lowest-class Putrid Scum.[24] What do you have to say about that?!

Pundit O. Gasbag

Wimpy Sham Radical: *[waveringly]* I kind of guess that's what I've been doing…I suppose, maybe.

Pundit O. Gasbag: How can you live with yourself? Don't you realize that those Putrid Scum normally would just starve in Homeless Alley because they're so dim-witted and lazy? The Emperor is doing them a favor by building posh new prisons for them. You're stupid, unpatriotic, and you disgust me!

---

24 Lott (2002) used the term "social distancing" to reveal the extent to which the poor face denigration and discrimination in our classist society. Social distancing discounts the character of impoverished people and thereby establishes serious barriers to their achievement while robbing them of equal opportunity. Some specific examples of the phenomenon take the form of derogatory terms such as crackers, okies, lintheads, and ridge runners as local designations for people who fall into the larger category of white trash. The media reinforces discrimination against the poor by portraying them as outsiders with deficient character (Bullock, Wyche, & Williams, 2001).

Shrilly Noxious: *[screeching]* You're absolutely right, Pundit!

Wimpy Sham Radical: *[hesitantly]* I suppose you might be right, possibly, perhaps. I'm not sure.

Shrilly Noxious: *[agitated, spitting, and shrieking]* Darn right he's right! I can't stand soft, mushy, spineless, treasonous bags of pus like you. If you ran the country, all the evildoers and degenerates from all over the Vassal Lands would take over and drive our glorious system into the ground! Why don't you just go jump off a bridge? And throw your kids off first because we don't want any more like you around!

Pundit O. Gasbag: *[bellowing]* You're absolutely, absolutely, absolutely right Shrilly![25]

Wimpy Sham Radical: *[traumatized]* Well, I don't know about a bridge— ummm, hmmm.

Pundit O. Gasbag: I guess we proved something here today! Before we bring in our next guest I want to remind our millions of loyal ditto-gasbag viewers and listeners that Shrilly and I both have new books on the *Taradiddle Times* best-seller list. Shrilly's book, *How and Where to Kick a Softie When He's Down,* will give you ideas about how to become more politically active in support of our wonderful Emperor. My book, titled *Gasbag's Guide to Glory Land,* will offer you many ways to make our utopian nation even more utopian. Shrilly, it's time for your daily values tirade. What do you have for us today?

Shrilly Noxious: Thanks Pundit. I'll be talking about some of the most disgusting behavior you'll ever encounter. *[wild eyed]* Of course, some of it is happening in the morally bankrupt Vassal Lands, but regrettably some of it is right here at home. In the nation of Altruistia, one of the Vassal Lands that we haven't yet conquered, their corrupt government has the audacity to tax everyone, even the wealthy, so they can support their ridiculous social

---

25 It's easy to spot weak thinking when pundits frequently shout out "You're absolutely right!" Right-wing talk-show hosts are notorious for proclaiming the correct thinking of "dittoheads" who call in agreeing with them. But complex issues usually entail shades of grey and require nuanced judgment instead of dogmatic certainty (Resnick, 1987). Very seldom is anyone absolutely right about anything, especially when dealing with a complex issue. Along similar lines, Tetlock (2005) drew from the work of Isaiah Berlin to distinguish between two kinds of experts—fox and hedgehog thinkers. Foxes flexibly draw from various viewpoints while hedgehogs are dominated by one big idea or a rigid ideology and impose a predetermined solution on complex, ill-defined problems. Of course foxes are superior solvers of complex problems. Tetlock identified an inverse relationship between good judgment and the single-minded dogmatism the media prefers in its pundits.

programs. You won't believe how they waste the taxpayers' money either. For one thing, they have universal health care so everyone can just walk into a doctor's office and get treatment regardless of what class they come from! I say, if they can't pay for it they don't deserve it! *[spitting and sputtering]* They also waste money on early childcare for all kids in the country, even the poorest! Think about it. Why should you or I pay for cookies and milk in posh daycare centers for someone else's hopeless, filthy, spoiled brats?!

And if you thought that was bad, just listen to this *[screaming and pounding the desk]*. The Altruistians are so evil and corrupt that they just passed an equal rights amendment to their constitution making women eligible for equal pay and giving them the same rights as men! Now as you can see I'm a woman, and a very attractive one at that, but I know that a culture will just collapse from within if you undermine the rights of the patriarchs! How can they protect traditional values if the great white fathers of the nation don't have the power to impose order? My daddy beat me all the time *[louder shrieking, eyes spinning in their sockets, animated desk pounding]*, but I knew that he was doing it to protect me from my own baser impulses. And he was right! Look how I turned out! I think the Altruistians are a foul blight on the moral fabric of the world and we have to do something about it! I hope the Emperor launches a nuclear attack on them to wipe this corruption off the map. And then we should ask Abominate Frenzy to go in and convert any survivors to the Maniacal Cult of Intolerant Absolutism!

One more thing, I mentioned that we have some problems at home. Did you know that we still have an opposition party in our federal government?! The Decrepit Reformist party still plans to run a few candidates in the next senatorial election, if there is another election. Of course, they won't stand a snowball's chance in hell of winning any seats in the senate, but the fact that they're still trying sends a chill up my spine. What if their evil, unpatriotic message gets through to some of our kids?! Do you want your kid thinking like a progressive?! I won't have it I tell you! I think it's high time that our Emperor bans all opposition parties so we don't ever have to worry about them again!

Exhausted, Shrilly stooped over the desk dripping sweat and panting. The rest of the show carried much the same tone. Pundit and Shrilly pilloried a feminist scholar, an environmentalist, and a group of mothers who were promoting early childcare for the poor. As a closer for the show they interviewed a politician who could have been Pundit's twin brother in stature, in demeanor, and certainly in belief. Many times, Pundit punctuated this last interview with his well-worn phrase, "You're absolutely right!" After the show, Spinner took me to the center of the nation's government, where I hoped to see the world's best legislators in action.

CH 5.

A TRIP TO LOBBYVILLE AND GOVERNMENT HOUSE

The domed government-house Capitol Building was a magnificent but crumbling old structure with a lofty rotunda at its center. A few pillars had fallen away and a few more were leaning precariously. The old carved marble government motto over the columns at the front of the rotunda read, "Protect our democracy at all costs!" But it was cracked and a few letters had broken away from the word "democracy." Workers were hoisting a new piece of gleaming, polished marble with the word "plutocracy" engraved into its face to replace the crumbling democracy section.[26] *Walking around behind the Capitol Building, we noticed an array of large, glitzy structures attached right to the back of the government-house. Each of these buildings had a flashy sign with the name and logo of a prominent corporation. One was named the "Stupor Drugs Pharmaceutical Lobby Headquarters." Another was the "Coughing Coal-Black Industries Lobbying Agency." Still others stood behind these impressive facilities.*

Prober: What are these buildings for? Why are they attached directly to the back of the government building?

---

26 All democracies in the modern world are imperfect and unjust to varying degrees because they all fail to provide equal freedom and opportunity for their citizens (Gutmann, 2003). Democratic governance is an unrealized ideal and we're either strengthening an imperfect version of it or letting it erode.

Spinner: These just might be the best evidence for our claim that we have the most efficient government in the world. Thousands of professional lobbyists work in them. Basically, their job is to make sure the elected politicians are held accountable.

Prober: Accountable to whom?

Spinner: Why the corporations paying the lobbyists' big salaries, of course. Who do you think?[27]

Prober: How does the lobbying work?

Spinner: It depends on the Corporate Protection Act: a law that makes it illegal to sue any corporation for any reason.[28] I'll tell you more about that law later but here's the gist of it for now. When our biggest oil and coal corporation, Coughing Coal-Black Industries, was facing some lawsuits from a few citizens and their sleazy personal injury lawyers who were whining about illnesses supposedly caused by coal-burning plants the executives of Coal-Black got on the blower and called up their lobbyists here at the capital. They

---

27 Democracy relies on the creation and maintenance of a healthy civil society in which well-informed citizens interact, communicate, and collaborate in political processes (Guttmann, 2003). According to Chambers (2002), "an unhealthy civil society is one that has been colonized by power or money or both" (p. 94). The proliferation of powerful lobbyists who manipulate and bribe politicians into actions that benefit an influential few interest groups represents pernicious colonization of civil society by money. Most lobbyists in Washington represent corporate and neoconservative interests (Hacker & Pierson, 2005); therefore, neoconservatives are undermining our democracy. While the majority of Americans are politically moderate, right-wing extremists including influential lobbyists have ignored the general will of the people while pushing our government far to the extreme right end of the ideological spectrum. Hacker and Pierson observed an interesting sign that our government has shifted far toward the extreme right wing. They noted that some key politicians who have maintained consistent ideological positions over the long term were considered right-wing extremists a few decades ago but are now considered moderates or even liberals because the ideological climate has pushed many other politicians past them in a mad rush toward the right. The same is occurring elsewhere. Monbiot (2000) worried about the end of representative democracy in Britain as corporate interests co-opt or undermine various government functions such as protection of consumers, regulation of the workplace, and conservation of the environment. The eminent political theorist Sheldon Wolin (2004, 2008) summed it up well, arguing that we have degenerated toward "inverted totalitarianism," a new political form dominated by economic power instead of political dynamics.

28 Similar to Hubris Mendacious of Neoconland, most politicians in America are so well controlled by corporate lobbyists (Hacker & Pierson) that a law approximating the Corporate Protection Act isn't that far-fetched.

told them what the problem was and said they needed some business-friendly legislation quick. The lobbyists got busy writing a bill outlawing lawsuits against corporations, ran it by the executives of Coal-Black for their approval, and then went to see the politicians they own in the Capitol Building. Come on in and I'll show you the hallowed halls that bind business and government together so seamlessly.

Prober: I see there's a big revolving door joining the Capitol Building with the Coughing Coal-Black Lobbying Agency.

Spinner: Yes, the revolving door gives the lobbyists easy access to the politicians. It works the other way too. When a politician loses an election, which almost never happens anymore,[29] or when he retires, he simply walks through the revolving door and joins the lobbying firm. Some of them go around and around, spending a few years lobbying and then running for election, and so on. A few of them rotate through the doors so fast that they end up lobbying themselves. Let's go up into the gallery in the rotunda. A legislative session is about to start so you'll get to see truly efficient plutocracy in action.

Making our way to the gallery seats, we could see several hundred politicians down below hooting, hollering, and throwing wads of paper at one another. A very old gentleman in the speaker's chair polished his spectacles, adjusted his unruly, white mane, and pounded his gavel, yelling out in a thick southern drawl, "Y'all better calm down and come to order now, Y'hear!" When the din subsided, a politician stood up awkwardly to speak.

Spinner: That's Senator Hubris Mendacious III Esquire. He comes from a very prominent family and he's been in lobbying and government for many years.

Prober: I notice that he moves awkwardly. Is he ill?

Spinner: He moves like that only when the lobbyists have their strings attached to him. Look closely and you'll notice some thin wires attached to metal eyehooks that are screwed into his knees, wrists, skull, larynx, and groin. Whenever a politician does anything significant, like introducing a bill to the legislature, or making a speech on Weasel News TV, the lobbyists who own him attach their puppet strings so they can make sure he stays on message.[30] One wrong move, and they jerk his strings, and that can be

---

29 Republican gerrymandering in recent years rigged district boundaries to favor Republican incumbent candidates in future elections. While gerrymandering has a long, sleazy track record, recent abuses stand out as particularly egregious (Hacker & Pierson, 2005; Wolfe, 2006).

30 Deception of the voting public pays big political dividends for the unscrupulous in our imperfect democracy (Hacker & Pierson; Mendelberg, 2001). For example, Mendelberg's research showed that prominent politicians routinely use subtle

painful. Sometimes it gets very interesting in here. When they're debating an important bill that could have an effect on one or more of our corporations, lobbyists stampede through the revolving doors, pour into the rotunda, attach their puppet strings to the politicians they own, and then come up here to these balconies to—well—pull some strings. When you watch the politicians down on the floor, it looks like the dance of the marionettes! Occasionally, the strings get tangled up but the result is always the same. Thanks to our strong lobbyists, the corporations always get their way, and that's always good for all of us all the time.

Prober: Don't the politicians get upset about the strings? How can they stand being manipulated like that?

Spinner: Well, just remember that most of them want to be lobbyists after they leave office. Or, they want lucrative positions in the executive offices or

boardrooms of the corporations that own the lobbyists. So you can see it's to their advantage to play along as puppets. Most politicians actually like to have their strings pulled because the lobbyists keep them from making big mistakes that might cost them cushy jobs as corporate figureheads in their later years. The puppet strings are a win-win for everyone. Hey, I have a surprise for you. I asked the lobbyists for the corporation that owns Senator Hubris Mendacious III Esquire if you could have a brief interview with him and they agreed. Let's go down to the floor of the rotunda to meet him.

After the legislative session, down on the rotunda floor I noticed that lobbyists were removing their puppet strings from politicians who were leaving the building. Due to our impending interview, Senator Mendacious still had his firmly attached.

Senator Hubris Mendacious III Esquire, with Lobbyist's Puppet Strings

racist messages to win the white vote. The Willie Horton advertisements during the successful presidential campaign of George H. W. Bush was a prominent example, because it stoked white racism through fear of violent crime.

Prober: It's an honor to meet you sir. Please tell me how you got into politics.

Hubris: Well, I come from a prominent family and my daddy raised me to be a politician. He always said, "Son, when you grow up you have to fight dirty to skim off more of the government money that made us rich... gurgle...aaargh!"[31]

Senator Mendacious gagged and stopped speaking due to an abrupt tightening of the puppet string attached to a metal ring embedded in his Adam's apple.

Hubris: Uh, I meant to say that I became a politician to protect family values, to grow the economy, and to fight the evildoers in the foreign Vassal Lands.

Prober: I hesitate to ask this, but what industry owns you?

Hubris: I'm proud to say that the people from Stupor Drugs own me lock, stock, and barrel and I do whatever they say...Ouch!

The senator jumped around in pain from a strong yank on the puppet string attached to his groin. In a somewhat higher voice he continued.

Hubris: I mean Greed is good! Dogma forever! More! More! Bigger! Bigger! At all costs! I'm sorry; I have an important event to get to. Emperor Ninny is giving his weekly directives to the nation in a few minutes. It was nice visiting with you, and remember to vote for me at the next election, if the Emperor decides to have another election, that is.

Prober: Wasn't Senator Mendacious III Esquire just quoting from the Golden Slab?

Spinner: Yes, and I'm glad he was. It proves he was worthy of winning his last election. I'm so proud to have him in our government.

Prober: He said the Emperor is giving a speech. Can we see it?

Spinner: Of course! In fact, it's wise to show up at his speeches. The patriotism you demonstrate by being in his audience sends a good message to all the secret police who are watching you. We just have to step out onto the lawn in front of this building because the Emperor makes most of his speeches from a balcony near the top of the rotunda.

Outside, the bright, noonday sun managed to cut through the grimy Fascisto smog. A large, gathering throng pressed in close to the Capitol Building. Burly young men wearing dark sunglasses and black suits were everywhere, outnumbered only by soldiers carrying automatic weapons. Within a few minutes, Emperor Bovine Ninny appeared on the balcony and a hush fell over the crowd.

---

31 According to Murphy (2007), there are some remarkable parallels between modern America and ancient Rome when it was poised on the brink of collapse. The runaway bribery and corruption in government and the confusion of private gain with public good through rampant privatization are two of the most informative similarities.

Emperor Bovine Ninny

Emperor Bovine: Hi all youse, uh, hmmm, citizens. As y'all know, I Emperor Bovine Ninny, just call me Bo, am the best Emperor we ever had and I'm glad youse know it. Since my good ol' boy friends at Coughing Coal-Black Industries made me into the Emperor, I've kept my business friends very happy. Burp! I know that cuz they tell me so every day, and they give me tons of cash. I'm the decider guy, the chooser guy, and figger-outer guy, cuz I figger out what to do to help my friends and then I decider tuh do it. So my other name is the figger-outer-decider guy, heh, heh. We've also invaded 6 Vassal Land countries since I took over. *[An aide stepped forward and whispered in his ear.]* I mean 12 countries. Hard tuh keep track, heh heh. I invaded them to make them be more demacritical and tuh be more like us. Yah know, they hate us fer our freedoms and they're real jealous becuz they don't have great leaders like we do. I think y'all should eat lots more meat becuz the slaughterhouses told me I should tell you tuh eat more. Snort! So go have a big slab of barbecued beast for breakfast tomorrow morning. I know I will. Oh, and by the way, if you see anyone acting all suspicious-like, snooping around and such, make sure y'all call the secret police and tell them about them evildoers. We can't be too careful y'know cuz there's lots of evildoers and they might try tuh kill ya, or even worse, they might try tuh take yer money! If I wasn't the Emperor there would be evildoers all over the place; at least that's what the think-tank guys say. There's less of them bad guys becuz I been huntin em down and smokin em out. That's cuz I'm real good at ferrin policy. One more thing. Make sure y'all vote fer me at the next election becuz it's good tuh vote fer heroes. *[The aide stepped forward and whispered in his ear again.]* Oh, ha, ha, I forgot that I decidered a while back not tuh have elections fer Emperor no more. Youse just vote fer the Senators and some other guys. Well, that's all I got tuh say becuz the Wildbelly Wrestlin starts soon on Weasel TV and I got tuh have a few more beers before the first smackdown. Wahoo! See y'all next week.

A deafening roar went up from the crowd. Most people were waving small Neoconland flags and rocking to and fro as chants of "Bovine! Bovine! Bovine!" erupted spontaneously.

Prober: I must say, I expected more from an Emperor. He really didn't say much and he certainly didn't say it well.

Spinner: Come on now. You saw how he connected with the people! You should be honored to be in his presence! Besides, it doesn't really matter if he's smart or not. He has handlers to do the thinking for him. I only wish we had more heroic leaders like him! Speaking of heroic leaders, we should go see some more of the great thinkers in our think-tank complex just down the road. Let's go.

Сн 6.

THOUGHTLESS THINK TANKS, FISHMEN, AND MIND EXCREMENT

Driving into the far-right side of Fascisto, we were confronted with an impressive sight. Stretching off into the distance were enormous open-top, glass tanks filled with murky water and interconnected with PVC plumbing pipes. Each tank was emblazoned with a magnificent, glowing neon sign.

Prober: These tanks have such interesting names. What's their purpose?

Spinner: They do a variety of impressive things to keep our corporations and politicians happy. This tank here is labeled the Glorious Birthright Foundation (GBF) because it protects the right of Blueblood families to own and control most of our financial institutions, and it protects them from taxation on their inheritances. Without the GBF our best families wouldn't have nearly as much money as they do now. The GBF fellows wrote the Bimbo Jumbobazoom Welfare Law that made taxation of inheritances illegal. They worked very quickly on that, getting their lobbyists to pull some political strings to ensure its passage and implementation in the Capitol Building. They named the statute after a wealthy heiress who derives great benefit from the Bimbo law. In fact, she stands to inherit over 100 billion lucre-buck dollars from her daddy. It would have been only 80 billion without the Bimbo law. Can you imagine what a difference that will make in her lifestyle?

Another think tank is the Neoconland Chicanery Institute (NCI), which makes sure everyone understands how awesome our corporations or our great Emperor are. The fellows of the NCI spring into action whenever some misguided fool raises an issue that might cause embarrassment to our corporate leaders or to the Emperor and his entourage. For example, when a few muddleheaded, old-school journalists dug up some documentation suggesting that our current emperor was a mentally challenged, drug-abusing alcoholic who flunked out of school and bumbled through most of his life in a stupor, the NCI wrote and publicized a position paper proving beyond the shadow of a doubt that his actions were caused by a decades-long case of food poisoning. I almost worked for the NCI a while back because they really liked my last name.

The Dissent Suppression Forum (DSF) is another think tank. It finds ways to silence any unpatriotic, backstabbing group that criticizes the way we do things here in Neoconland. Most lowlifes now know that they have to speak well of our leaders—or else! The DSF has ruined many a charlatan's career. By the way, it should come as no surprise that Shrilly Noxious, the Weasel News commentator you saw earlier, works closely with that think tank.

Yet another is the Superficial Surface Skimming (SSS) think tank, which does a marvelous job of finding ways to clarify the most complex problems so our politicians can recommend simple, black-and-white solutions for highly complicated issues. For example, when bleeding-heart liberals kept arguing that street crime emerges from a complex combination of factors such as racial and class-based segregation, crushed aspirations, under-funded public education, a lack of rewarding employment opportunities, easy access to guns, and other influences, the SSS conclusively proved that lower-class criminals are demonic evildoers—simple, done, case closed, game over, no more need to think about it.

One more think tank is the Skeptical Septic Tank (SST), which trains its smart, young fellows to think and act like scientists so they can go on Weasel News TV talk shows to refute any complaints from those sicko environmentalists.[32] There are many other tanks. I could go on and on.[33]

---

32 Our society's love of radical individualism, for which the neoconservatives are the loudest cheerleaders, has been a major driving force behind the environmental devastation that plagues our era (Ferkiss, Bergmann, Agarwal, & Floro, 1993). Individuals concerned with short-term personal gain have trouble appreciating the long-term, widespread consequences of their actions.

33 A small but wealthy and well-connected conservative elite came to dominate the social and political agendas of America over the past few decades. A major tool for this commandeering of our culture has been the establishment of think tanks and foundations that promote a radical neoconservative social and economic agenda (Halper & Clark, 2004; Stefancic & Delgado, 1996). The think

It was hard to tell what was in the muddy waters of the tanks. Stepping closer and pressing our faces up against the DSF tank, we could make out a number of rapidly swimming creatures wearing soggy but upmarket blazers or three-piece, pinstripe suits and tightly holding expensive, leather briefcases. As one of these creatures, or "fellows" as Spinner called them, swam close to our side of the tank, I was surprised to see that it looked like a man-fish hybrid. Its face was markedly human but it had gills and scales. Its arms were shaped like rudimentary fins, its feet were webbed, and there was a lengthy fish tail growing from the back of its expensive trousers. On the floor of the tank below the swimmers we could see a mucky sludge buildup about three feet deep. The plumbing pipes connected the tanks with one another and with some facilities outside the think-tank complex. The pipes seemed to be sucking the sludge from the tanks, mixing it together throughout the complex, and distributing it to other locations in Neoconland. The largest conduit traversed over a hill toward Fascisto and funneled directly into the headquarters of Weasel News. Other pipes headed toward other important locations in Fascisto including the Emperor's mansion, the Capitol Building rotunda, the Zealots' Court Building, the Rubber Stamp Senate building, and of course the darkened back-room offices of Lobbyville. A few more pipes extended away to various locations elsewhere in the nation.

Equally interesting, on the southwestern edge of the complex hovered the summit of Mt. Exclusion, which was draped with the magnificent pillars, flying buttresses, and ornate hallways of the prestigious Dogma University. Slides extended downward from the university to diving boards on the think tanks.

Prober: What an interesting place. Please tell me about these tanks.

Spinner: This is the heart of the nation. The fellows in these tanks generate the best legal and economic ideas for distribution throughout the land. Have a look at the fellow on the diving board at the edge of the DSF tank. He's a recent graduate of the Dogma University Graduate School of

---

tanks carry out "research" violating the rules of objectivity that real scholarly research must follow. A common practice is the hiring of unscrupulous, semi-credentialed intellectuals to write position papers and make media appearances conveying ideas favorable to the corporations and powerful ideologues who hire them (Lipsitz, 2000). Consequently, they establish the illusion of unbiased "discoveries" while "proving" their foregone, ideologically tainted conclusions. Largely due to think tanks, the popular view is that unregulated free-market capitalism creates wealth for all while also promoting democracy. But Hodgson (2004) cut through the ideological deception to reveal ways in which the severe and growing economic inequality of recent decades approximates the worst class stratification and power imbalances of old Europe.

Legalese Economics.[34] He just slid down the career-path chute from the university to the diving board and he's ready to immerse himself in a career as a DSF fellow. As a think-tank hatchling, he'll learn to swim around adding his ideological mind droppings to the fudge-like paste in the bottom of the tank. A few critics have called the stuff "sludge," but don't listen to them. It's paste and it's marvelous, as you'll soon see. Have a look at that blowhole on the top of the fellow's head. Every now and then a think-tank fellow forcefully expels a load of ideological mind excrement from the blowhole, thus dumping more paste into the tank. As the ideological paste accumulates, the pipes transport it around the complex to mix with the paste of the other tanks. When mixed and refined, the paste becomes idea fuel for use throughout the land. It operates much like a drug—a judgment-improving opiate of the mind so to speak. The think-tank operators discovered that mixing the mind-excrement of these fishmen fellows and then distributing it throughout the nation creates a very favorable ideological climate. Constant exposure to ideological paste over a long period of time can make the majority of the population quite open-minded and willing to accept just about any message the fellows want to convey. It's a pretty good bet that Weasel News couldn't operate without the 1300 gallons of ideological paste idea fuel it consumes daily to generate its inspirational news stories about our angelic heroes and the wonderful things we do in the world, or the terrifying stories about the evildoer foreigners from the Vassal Lands.

Prober: *[incredulous]* The think-tank fellows spew crap out of blowholes in the top of their heads?! How is that possible? And why do they come to look like fish in the first place?

Spinner: Oh please don't call it crap! It's our mind fuel—wonderful stuff. Morphing into fishmen is an aspect of the career the fellows willingly accept. If you're going to swim for several decades in this kind of tank you have to adapt. Just as sharks must swim incessantly to stay alive, the fellows must dump their mind excrement regularly and agitate the neoliberal waters incessantly to mix the ideological paste in the bottom of the tanks, refining it into thought fuel for distribution throughout the land. But the School of Legalese Economics in Dogma University does a great job of preparing them. It gives them regular transfusions, draining away much of their warm human blood and injecting large quantities of cold-shark, economic blood to make them fit for life in the tank.

---

34 Many of the most active right-wing extremists emerge from law schools that are saturated with neoconservative ideology (see Sunstein, 2005). The University of Chicago Law School is the most infamous example.

Gil Flounderfib: Fellow at the Glorious Birthright Foundation Think Tank

In addition, the fellows undergo genetic mutation in the sociobiology[35] school of the university and this enables them to grow the gills, scales, fins,

---

35 The field of sociobiology promotes social Darwinism, which provides a useful theoretical framework for neoconservative thought and action. See the related footnote number 40 in this chapter for a discussion of social Darwinism as it applies to class distinctions.

and tails they need to swim constantly in the ideological water. The blowholes came about accidentally. During their ideological genetic mutation at Dogma University, a bit of whale DNA somehow got into the system and the fellows developed these blowholes. I hear they work something like this. As a fellow thinks and thinks and thinks and thinks and thinks really hard about how to put a neocon spin on an issue it generates a high-pressure buildup of mind excrement. When the pressure gets to a certain point it blasts out of the blowhole in a spectacular brown eruption. It was a surprise to everyone when this started happening but now it's commonplace. Many people in the nation love drinking in the stuff, especially our politicians and the journalists over at Weasel News. See that fellow over there getting ready to jump back in the tank? That's Gil Flounderfib, one of the most prolific correctors of history in the think-tank complex. He takes the history books written by the biased, liberal historians from the old universities and corrects their mistakes and distortions to ensure that we all know the truly accurate history of Neoconland. And he adds some real flair to his work. You should have seen the bonfire when he sponsored a book burning of all the old, inaccurate history texts.

Anyway, Gil has spectacular mind-excrement explosions. As a member of the Glorious Birthright Foundation his eruptions generated the life-story series that glorified our Emperors and endeared them to the public. He also produced the policy papers that justified some of our most magnificent wars back when we actually needed justification to start a war. He sure dumps a lot of sludge, er, I mean paste into the GBF tank!

Prober: Can you tell me more about what these tanks have accomplished over the years?

Spinner: A lot! They've changed the minds of millions on many important issues. For example, with the help of some new regulators in our science research complex, the Neoconland Chicanery Institute (NCI) was able to change opinion about global warming so that our industries could remain productive and highly profitable for their shareholders. A few years ago, the NCI silenced hundreds of so-called leading scientists from the old research universities we used to have—you know, the biased ones that operated on what they called objective, empirical science, whatever that meant. Anyway, those hundreds of biased scientists were running around frantically like Chicken Littles warning about the effects of global warming, saying that sea levels would rise, ocean currents would change, storms and droughts would increase, and so on. The NCI gave a promising young lobbyist by the name of Spurious Rhetoric several million lucre-buck dollars in grant money to develop a counterargument, which he did. Mr. Rhetoric wrote a book titled *Cool Times on a Hot Earth,* which promoted the benefits of global warming. The chapters of the book had clever titles such as "Looking Forward to Nice,

Warm Summers," "Your Desert Home Might Become Valuable Ocean-Front Property," and "Who Cares About Penguins Anyway?" Several chapters in the book also listed the harm it would cause to industrial profits if we tried to control the pollution that causes global warming.[36] Weasel News

---

36 The overwhelming consensus of climate scientists points toward widespread, profound climate change (Flannery, 2006) even though neoconservative ideologues attempt to manufacture and trumpet an opposing view to protect business interests from the need to take social responsibility (Hansen, 2005). Much of the neoconservative skepticism about global warming comes from political hacks masquerading as climate experts and the tendency of the Bush administration to ignore, manipulate, and distort the findings of scientific research (Shulman, 2007). Thousands of credible scientists have been protesting this political manipulation of science (Shulman). In spite of the implausibility of their position, the global warming skeptics' counterarguments are effective because TV talk shows habitually attempt to create a balanced debate between representatives of "both sides." The public gets the impression that the weight of evidence for the two sides of the issue are about equal even though the neoconservative represents a weak, minority view and the opposing scientist represents a large collection of credible, objective scientists who have accumulated an overwhelming array of evidence. This is the same immoral and highly effective corporate spin strategy that the cigarette companies have used for decades to deceive the public and block regulation of their toxic product (see Brandt, 2007). Prominent scholars certainly are concerned about climate change and other aspects of environmental damage. The eminent biologist E. O. Wilson (2002) stressed that human commerce and development are generating a mass extinction of living species beyond anything since the mass extinction of the dinosaurs. Synthesizing a large interdisciplinary body of research, and using examples of nations and cultures from ancient to modern times, Diamond (2004) found patterns in our current behaviors that could generate devastating environmental collapse on a massive scale. He described how earlier civilizations such as the Maya of Central America and the Anasazi of the American Southwest, among others, collapsed largely due to self-imposed resource shortages and environmental degradation. Diamond argued that current environmental abuses generated by our runaway economic systems have us on a path toward similar societal collapses, which could be accompanied by starvation, disease epidemics, widespread warfare, and genocide. Speth (2004) showed how these large-scale collapses can come in the form of rapid crashes rather than gradual

interviewed Mr. Rhetoric several times a day, every day for five years straight and advertised his book vigorously. Before you knew it, this one scientist had defeated hundreds of supposedly knowledgeable scientists in the court of public opinion. The wimpy scientists who were scared of global warming went home with their tails between their legs.

Prober: You called Spurious Rhetoric a scientist but before that you said he was a lobbyist.

Spinner: Actually, he has a BA in duplicity with a minor in obfuscation, and he got his start as a lobbyist for Coughing Coal-Black Industries. He may not be a real scientist but he sure sounds like one and that's what counts.

Prober: But global warming has been causing a lot of problems. There have been widespread storm surges along with flooding in coastal regions around the world. Hurricanes and tornadoes are a lot more frequent and powerful now. The droughts are devastating, destroying crops in many nations and causing massive famines. Millions of people in the Vassal Lands starved to death in the big drought. Didn't thousands of Neoconians lose their homes in Hurricane Unnecessary last year?[37]

Spinner: Why should we care about what happens in the Vassal Lands? That was their problem. And the ones who lost their homes here in Neoconland? It was their own fault that their trailers and rickety apartments were destroyed. They shouldn't live in those flimsy trailers anyway. They should build the concrete-bunker McMansions that the Splendiferous Bluebloods and Insatiable Predators live in. Those houses resist all hurricanes and they have great air conditioning so the heat doesn't bother you. And most important, they should have prayed harder in Abominate Frenzy's megachurch services. If they were responsible individuals they would have been OK.

---

decline. They would be characterized by resource shortages, habitat destruction for animals and humans, epidemics, mass poverty, and social chaos.

37 The Bush administration downplayed the reality of climate change for years while replacing highly qualified professionals in government departments with much less qualified political cronies. These replacements included the leaders of FEMA, which is responsible for disaster relief. In the aftermath of Hurricane Katrina, thousands of people remained stranded for long periods of time and many died due to the poor emergency response (Baker, 2007).

Neoconian Currency: The Lucre-Buck Dollar

Prober: You mentioned Dogma University. Interesting name! What degrees can you get from that institution?

Spinner: There are bachelors and advanced degrees in venality, collusion, knavery, and the perfidious arts, among others. But don't expect to just pick up a degree. Not just anyone can "get" a degree there. You have to be the right kind of person from good stock. Then you have to pass the admission exam and the genetic screening. On the exam, there are some questions testing reading, writing, and 'rithmetic ability. But most importantly, you have to know the history of Neoconland inside and out. Who are our heroes and what did they do? How did some of these heroes vanquish their evil, liberal enemies to create our utopian society? Can you recite the Golden Slab word for word?[38] Things like that. The college entrance exam screens out most of the riffraff but the genetic testing makes absolutely certain that only the right candidates get in.

Prober: How so?

Spinner: Legacy Library in the university collects the genetic code of every citizen in the nation and every code fits into a layered category system so we can keep track of who fits in which social class.[39] You may have noticed that

38 Some neoconservatives have been attempting to force universities into compliance with their ideology (see Neufield & Strickland, 1995) by attacking academic freedom and advocating legislation that would force universities to magnify the influence of right-wing professors (e.g., Horowitz, 2006). The logical end point would entail dismantling universities and creating a centralized, replacement institution driven completely by dogma.

39 McKinnon (2005) argued that much theory in evolutionary psychology is shaped by neoliberal (i.e., neoconservative) economic values, which create misleading survival of the fittest socioeconomic myths justifying extreme exploitation and inequality as the results of human nature. Through extensive, in-depth studies of primate behavior, de Waal (2006; Aureli & de Waal, 2000) revealed that nature

I mentioned some of our classes once or twice before. The few Splendiferous Bluebloods are at the top followed by the Insatiable Predator[40] class. The bottom classes are by far the largest including the working-class Near Dregs and, at the very bottom, the Putrid Scum. Some of the Putrid Scum work but most are homeless or in prison. You may have noticed the wrist tattoos every citizen wears. These are stamped at birth. The Bluebloods have a small navy blue drop tattoo. The Insatiable Predators have a tattoo of blood-red canine teeth. The Near Dregs have a large skull and crossbones, and the Putrid Scum wear a large toxic waste symbol that covers the entire wrist.[41]

---

itself makes much room for cooperative, altruistic behavior alongside survival of the fittest competition. Wilson (1978) concurred, arguing that considerable research and theory in sociobiology shows that societies can be humane and egalitarian without violating evolutionary theory. Consequently, the inclination to justify harsh, aggressive dominance and exploitation in Neoconland as "just human nature" is inaccurate and creates a socioeconomic system that is more barbaric and cruel than typical behaviors in the "primitive" animal world.

40 The Insatiable Predator class reflects the neoconservative love of social Darwinism as a pseudo-scientific justification for the ways in which their ideology promotes the conscience-free exploitation of others. Social Darwinism is a recurring, dubious overextension of biological Darwinian theory that portrays as natural aggressive competition among humans and the subsequent layering of human populations into merit-based hierarchies (see Rose, 1998). The corollary is that little can or should be done to redress gross inequalities and injustices because such attempts would violate the essence of human nature. Nevertheless, major ethical problems ensue from blind application of social Darwinism. First, even if the theory is on the mark, and many prominent scholars insist it is not, why should we assume that our baser, animal nature should prevail? Why shouldn't we employ our ethical awareness and higher-level thought capacities to mollify our exploitative actions instead of celebrating them? Second, why assume that our hierarchies reflect true merit? Many of those in the top levels of a class-based hierarchy lack merit because they were born into privilege. Many others ruthlessly clawed over others on their way to the top. Do we really want our merit reward system to honor lazy inheritors of privilege and the most psychopathological among us?

41 The prevalence of class distinctions in a society brings forth notions of justice. According to Cupit (1997), injustice comes from the unfitting treatment of people as if they are worth much less regard than they really deserve. It represents a pernicious form of unjustified contempt and disrespect for the basic worthiness of other human beings. In Neoconland, the putrid-scum tattoo also symbolizes the human penchant for demonizing other races, religions, or classes as inhuman freaks. Strickland (2003) illustrated the extremes to which such demonization can extend. For example, crusaders of the Middle Ages were encouraged to believe that Jews were demonlike, Tartars were cannibalistic, and Saracens had

Prober: *[puzzled]* Why the tattoos?

Spinner: Well, for one thing they make employment screening much easier. Employers just ask job candidates to show their wrists and this narrows down the candidate pool in a matter of seconds. Talk about efficiency! The tattoos also help make other aspects of our lives easier. For example, they help our prosecutors decide what to do in legal cases. At the beginning of an arraignment the judge asks to see the wrist tattoo of a defendant. The Putrid Scum and the Near Dregs go into the Shoddy track of the system while the Insatiable Predators go into the Boutique-Zenith track. The Splendiferous Bluebloods' cases are dismissed outright because they're superior people incapable of committing a crime. The Putrid Scum end up in front of Quick-and-Dirty judges who run through the cases very quickly because they know how to convict evil people with great efficiency. The Near Dregs typically face Rubber-Stamp judges who also convict quickly but take a little longer to assess the merits of the case. The few Insatiable Predators whose cases move forward are treated with kid gloves, befitting their station in life, because they are high-quality people. Can you see how the tattoos add so much efficiency to our judicial system? They also decide who gets into certain restaurants or theaters, and they show people where to sit in sports arenas. The Splendiferous Bluebloods and most of the Insatiable Predators sit in luxury boxes while the rest go to the nosebleed sections or into standing room in the end zones. The tattoos also make airport check-in and security screening much more efficient. You'll see that in action when you fly home at the end of your trip. You are flying home, aren't you?

Prober: Yes, I plan to. I arrived by boat because the global warming storms grounded all the planes between the Neutral Lands and here.

Spinner: We should head out of town now. We're going to Big Boxica, the commercial and financial hub of the nation, but on the way we'll visit the Atomistian people in Marketopia and Selfish Valley where they play a very interesting game called Neoclassicon.

---

animal heads and bodies. Lott (2002) showed how we apply similar forms of denigration to the poor in today's culture.

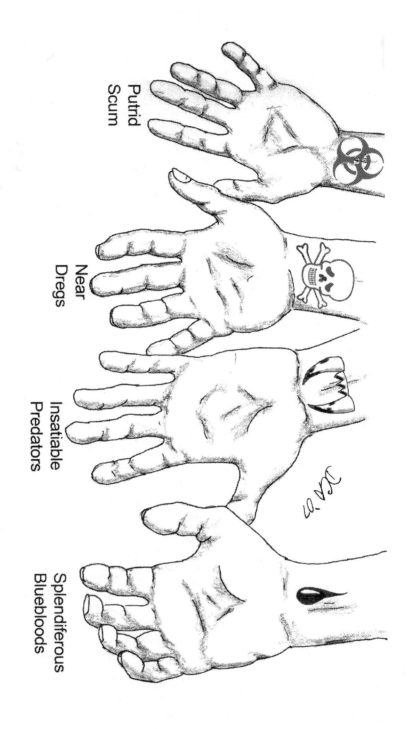

Wrist Tattoos for Efficient Class Distinction

Putrid
Scum

Near
Dregs

Insatiable
Predators

Splendiferous
Bluebloods

---------------- CH 7. ----------------

A GIANT, NEARLY INVISIBLE HAND IN MARKETOPIA AND SELFISH VALLEY

As we left Fascisto I gained my first glimpse of the rural countryside of Neoconland. Most of the hills were covered with tree stumps from clear-cut logging. In the plains, abandoned, dilapidated family farmhouses punctuated the cropland every half mile or so. We passed enormous factory farms with huge barns packed full of caged livestock.[42] We had to time our passage by these farms because large cannons periodically fired liquefied manure far out into the fields as fertilizer, and thousands of gallons were splattering the highway as if launched from huge, filthy lawn sprinklers run amok. Soon we descended into Selfish Valley toward the town of Marketopia, which was known as the birthplace of economic fundamentalism and the inspiration for most of the think tanks that now dominate the life of the nation. From the rim of the valley, Marketopia looked like a giant, concrete game board with squares marked off and painted various colors. Some box-shaped houses were being moved around constantly from one square to another while others were being dismantled and still others were being expanded. People were moving from square to square like game pieces, picking up prizes from piles of trinkets that were strategically located throughout the town.

---

42 Legislation ostensibly designed to support small family farmers actually hurts them and drives them off the land while enriching affluent, agribusiness corporations that run large-scale factory farms (see Gates & Collins, 2004).

Prober: Who are these people and what are they so busy doing?

Spinner: They're Atomistians who live here in Marketopia. Atomistians are very purposeful. They play an intensely serious, lifelong game of chase and gain, attempting to collect as many trinkets as possible along with the biggest box-houses they can get to store those trinkets.[43] They call the game Neoclassicon.

Prober: What kinds of trinkets are they after?

Spinner: Oh, just about anything. They collect shoes and suits, many more than they could ever wear in a lifetime. A big favorite is jewelry. One important objective of the game is to have larger jewels than any of your neighbors. If someone gets a big diamond or ruby for example, everyone else must go out and get one bigger. They love collecting vehicles, the bigger the better. That's one reason why Larceny Motors came up with the gigantic Earth Devastators you've seen on the road. Other trinkets are paintings, sculptures, fancy home entertainment systems, you name it. The Atomistians call their collections of trinkets piles-o-treasure. It's a fascinating game. If you watch for a while you'll see some Atomistians managing to collect large piles-o-treasure and enormous box-houses to store them in. When they do, it gets pretty funny. They'll climb to the top of their box houses and crow like roosters—"My pile-o-treasure is way bigger than your pathetic little piles." That seems to make all of them redouble their efforts and play the game even

---

43 Sociologist Amitai Etzioni (1993; 2001) lamented America's obsession with materialistic pursuits, arguing that we need more community and political involvement to address our persistent social problems. Applied to the realm of human thought and action, the term atomism implies individuality taken to the extreme. Atomistic individuals, such as the Atomistians of Selfish Valley, see themselves as self-encapsulated and self-interested, separated from the rest of humanity and concerned only with their own needs and wants. Philosopher Mary Midgley (2000) argued that atomism is a flawed philosophical and political assumption that magnifies an empty form of individualism while diminishing the important social aspects of our lives from which healthier forms of individuality arise. Stivers (2003) agreed, claiming that psychological egoism weakens us individually and collectively, making us fearful of others and vulnerable to totalitarianism. Excessive atomistic individualism distorts our lives by producing a vulgar, conflict-ridden, excessively materialistic world. Etzioni (1993) argued that we need to re-emphasize community to balance social responsibility with our excessive emphasis on individual rights. Sternberg (2001; 2005), a leading psychologist, argued that wisdom requires balancing one's own interests with the needs of others. In view of these considerations, the Atomistians lack wisdom even if some of them may be very clever.

harder. Many of them don't get any rest and some expire from the effort of the game. They don't stop until they drop.[44]

Prober: How do you get into the game? How do you become a player?

Spinner: You have to have seed capital to get the biggest box-houses and the biggest piles-o-treasure. A few players start with nothing and come close to winning but that's as rare as winning the lottery.[45] The best way in is to make sure you're born into a family that will give you a lot of playing chips when you start up as a player. But the game really separates winners from losers. Some collect many, many trinkets. Others gather a few cheap little things. Then they go to their little boxes and put the things inside. Notice that some have huge, fancy boxes far bigger than what they need to store the things they collect. Others have mid-size boxes, although their numbers have been dwindling; many others have tiny boxes tacked together with scrap

---

44 Ringmar (2005) observed that people are much more than just rational, economic actors and human life cannot be reduced to market transactions. Segal (1999) escaped our infatuation with economic growth and personal, materialistic wealth to advance an alternative vision. Noting that the good life is difficult to find, even for "winners" in the neoclassicon game, he advocated a shifting of priorities toward simplicity, which would emphasize beauty, generosity, peace of mind, and healthy social safety nets. According to some interesting research on the values embraced in differing societies, Segal's vision may be materializing to some extent. Discovering patterns in a massive data set from the World Values surveys, Inglehart (1997, 2000) reported a strong movement away from modern-materialist values toward postmodern-postmaterialist values in developed nations. Societies and individuals caught up in modern materialism seek material gain and follow rational-legal values in which legal frameworks and bureaucratic norms guide decision making. In contrast, those guided by postmodern postmaterialism embrace diversity, self-expression, aesthetics, and humanist considerations over economic growth and bureaucratic rationality.

45 The single-minded neoconservative economic emphasis on free markets with little government regulation has benefited only the wealthy few (Massey, 2005). More visionary economists recommend healthy government regulation of a still free market because too much "economic freedom" delivers neither widespread prosperity nor fairness, and it has caused profound harm (Galbraith, 1967, 1996; Veblen, 1994; Waligorski, 1997). Legal theorists Ackerman and Alstott (1999) argued that several decades of trickle-down economics promoted by neoconservatives has failed while aggravating already severe economic inequality in America. They claim that every citizen has the right to share in wealth created by previous generations, not just the offspring of the wealthy. Consequently, they recommend providing every young citizen a stake of $80,000, which would go a long way toward creating *true* equality of opportunity. This seed capital for human potential would be paid for by a 2% tax on wealth, which would come from the assets of the wealthiest 41% of the population.

board and corrugated tin. Still others have no boxes at all but then they don't have any trinkets to store in them anyway. If they can't afford a box on the game board for more than a few weeks, they're either flicked off the board onto a discard pile or they are sent to Homeless Alley over by the big prison complex. You'll see that later.

Prober: I see that some of them are wearing strange headpieces that sort of look like big rear-view mirrors attached to headbands.

Spinner: They're wearing the Self-Infatuation and Traditional-Values Rear-View Mirror. Atomistians now call it the Vainglory mirror. It's the latest fashion statement, and it's not only for looks. It has some very important practical value. You'll likely see advertisements for it on Weasel TV. It just came out but there are signs that it'll become very popular, not just in Atomistia.

Prober: Very interesting. But what is it for?

Spinner: Being very patriotic, Atomistians take the Golden Slab very seriously, especially the first commandment: "With thine own self be infatuated obsessively." Consequently, they spend a lot of time primping in the mirror and it detracts from the time they can devote to playing the game of Neoclassicon. So an enterprising fellow by the name of Facile Blinkerman invented the SITV mirror, got a couple of prominent Atomistians to wear them for a while and they caught on. If you take a closer look at one you'll notice that the mirror has zones something like trifocal glasses. The center part is called the self-infatuation magnification zone because it reflects the image of the wearer back, magnifying it and removing any blemishes or other flaws. The mirror also superimposes an etched lucre-buck dollar sign in the middle of the owner's face to reinforce the Atomistian's life purpose. The outside zones of the mirrors show the owners where they've been and where they came from on the game board while preventing them from seeing the path ahead. The mirrors do that because the Atomistians also like to honor the 10th commandment of the Golden slab—"Protect family values." By only looking behind themselves at the past they ensure the preservation of traditional values. The left side of the mirrors are fogged over for some reason, so the wearers only use the right side to navigate their way around the giant game board. Fortunately, they have to turn right as they turn each corner on the board, so steering themselves by looking in the rear-view mirror seems to work out. They always turn right, never left. You'll notice one more thing on the SITV mirrors. They have built-in earphones so the wearers can listen to Weasel News 24/7.

We watched the game for a while, and it was indeed rather comical. The players were scurrying around the board frantically grasping for trinkets. Many of them were having trouble carrying their prizes and were agonizing over trinkets that fell from their overburdened arms. As others pounced on fallen jewels and

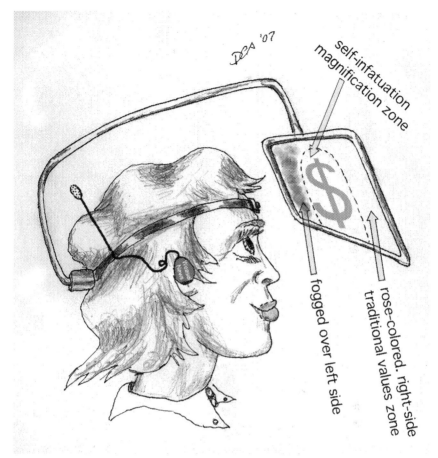

self-infatuation
magnification zone

fogged over left side

rose-colored, right-side
traditional values zone

Atomistian Wearing Self-Infatuating Traditional Values Rear-View Mirror

shoes bitter arguments ensued. In some cases, the arguments escalated to the point where the antagonists dropped all their trinkets and started slapping each other, pulling hair, tearing clothes, and shrieking at the top of their lungs. Of course, still other players swooped in on the dropped trinkets and skittered away with them before the arguments broke up.

Suddenly something unbelievable startled us, shaking the entire game board and knocking us off our feet. An enormous, translucent, nearly invisible, disembodied fist came swooping down from the sky and smashed some of the smallest box-houses, scattering splintered lumber, shattered glass, and piles-o-treasure all over the board. Then the fist relaxed, extended its fingers and started to gently scrape the scattered treasure toward the largest box-houses. Every now and then it would stop to flick a few Atomistians with its enormous index finger, sending them flying off the board into a discard heap of broken bodies. When finished it gently waved to the remaining players and hoisted itself high into the clouds from whence it came. As we watched it ascend, I noticed that its fingers were attached by giant cables to what looked like tall concrete towers in the hills beyond Selfish Valley.

Prober: What in the world was that?!

Spinner: I should have warned you. That's the invisible hand of Neoclassicon. It's the most important part of the game. According to the Atomistians, the giant hand reacts to the many moves of the players on the board and when certain patterns of play emerge, it drops down from the sky to make changes in the game. But it doesn't happen often—only when the small-time players start working cooperatively, banding together to counterbalance the huge advantage enjoyed by the big operators in the game.[46]

Prober: Why would they play a game with a gigantic, invisible fist hanging over them?

Spinner: Actually, the Atomistians like the hand because much of the time it's an open hand, not a fist. They say it makes the game fair and rewards the most deserving. Overall, they say it works out for the benefit of all players.

Prober: Except the ones whose box-houses were smashed, and those who were flicked off the board into the discard heap!

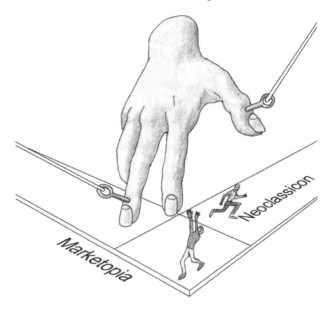

Adam Smith's Tethered Invisible Hand

---

46   There is a long history of union busting in America. Strategies ranging from anti-union legislation, to spying, to outright violence by federal soldiers and mercenary armies have been used to erode the influence and life chances of working-class people (see Norwood, 2002).

Spinner: Even they think it's a fair game. They often say so.

Prober: They say so? If they can still talk while they lie broken and bleeding on the heap. Why does the giant hand have strings attached to its fingers? I noticed big strings leading to those towers over the horizon.

Spinner: Oh, that was an improvement to the game made during the Great Privatization when our first Emperor was in power and he sold off the government to the corporations. The giant hand used to float around free operating on its own and everyone worried about that. The think-tank fellows along with the lobbyists and their corporate owners wanted to refine the game a little so they built those large control towers to tether the hand and guide its movements. The lobbyists from Lobbyville back in Fascisto own one tower. The think-tank fellows we visited earlier operate the other tower. Anyway, only the most powerful lobbyists and think-tank fellows work in the control towers. Whenever they think the Neoclassicon game needs a tweak or a nudge, they lower the hand to the game board and manipulate its fingers by pulling the strings with levers and pulleys. Only the top-echelon controllers know exactly how, when, and why the strings are pulled.[47]

Prober: Is that why the giant hand breaks up the paltry piles-o-treasure of the small players and scrapes them toward the larger houses?

Spinner: Could be, maybe, maybe not. As I say, only the controllers in the towers know for sure. Anyway, we should hike up to the top of the ridge on the other side of the valley to get a better look at the game.

---

47 The game Neoclassicon approximates the wild excesses of free-market fundamentalism, unregulated by government but manipulated by corrupt lobbyists and Wall Street insiders. The collapse of the financial system in 2008 and the subsequent demand for enormous government bailouts for Wall Street while Main Street suffered miserably were symptomatic of Adam Smith's manipulated invisible hand/fist. Moreover, such operations of Smith's fist also represent manifestations of the *shock doctrine* and *disaster capitalism* as articulated by Naomi Klein (2008). In the case of the actions on the large Neoclassicon game board, the enormous fist pounds the board to shock, stun, and destabilize the targeted players, and then robs them blind before they can recover.

CH 8.

ADAM SMITH CRAWLS FROM HIS GRAVE

After climbing out of Selfish Valley we looked back at the Neoclassicon game board. The large box-houses and piles-o-treasure seemed a little bigger than before and the discard body pile was significantly larger. And sure enough, as we peered up into the clouds at the giant, nearly invisible hand we could discern the periodic tensing of the think-tank and lobbyist cables shifting the hand to and fro and occasionally curling it into a rapidly descending fist. Tired from our climb, we stopped at an overgrown cemetery on a forested ridge still overlooking Selfish Valley. Wandering through the cemetery we come across a very strange sight. A dignified but musty, old, partially decomposed 18th-century Scottish gentleman was climbing out of his grave and frowning disdainfully at the scene in the valley below.

Spinner: What an honor! Do you know who this is, or rather was? Say hello to Adam Smith, the eminent 18th-century economist who forever changed the way we think about commerce and human destiny. That gigantic semi-invisible hand you saw flicking people and goods about in the town of Marketopia and Selfish Valley was his creation! All the neocon leaders view him as nothing less than a God! Let's go over and see if he'll talk with us a little.

Prober: I've certainly heard of him!

Spinner: Hello, Mr. Smith. Welcome to the 21st century. We're great admirers of your work and we wonder if you would visit with us a few minutes.

Smith: *[grumbling]* Aye laddies. Have a seat on those tombstones and take a look at what those brigands, hallions, and scoundrels are doing with my invisible hand! They're swinging it about wildly, destroying the work of the little people while scraping most of the treasure into the largest piles. It's made me turn over and over in my grave for the past few decades, so I just had to crawl back out to see if I can do something about it.

Spinner: *[incredulous]* You're unhappy with what's going on in Selfish Valley?!

Adam Smith Crawling from His Grave

Smith: Aye! Most people think I was an economist only, but I also was a philosopher concerned with ethics and moral behavior.[48] My invisible hand

---

48 Neoconservatives revere neoclassical economists because the latter invoke Adam Smith as a near divine early economist whose invisible hand of the marketplace justified extreme forms of self-interest and freedom from government regulation

was designed to free the people from control by the elite property owners and aristocrats who ran the nations in my time. It did that and still does to some extent. But I didn't intend for it to become a tool of just another elite with vile, rotten, black hearts. I cannot abide the way the powerful tie legal strings to it that favor them and hurt others. It's supposed to be a fair and generally benevolent hand that guides the market for the benefit of all who work diligently. I detest the way they manipulate it, making it curl into an iron fist that smashes the lives of the very people it was designed to help.

Spinner: Really? Please excuse us but we don't quite understand.

Smith: Notice that most people it crushes are not wealthy, and those it benefits most are born into privilege. Now some of the privileged are fine people but many of the most despicable, unscrupulous, greedy scoundrels are the true beneficiaries of my invisible hand in today's world. They inherit the levers of power or come to control them through skullduggery, and they make political and economic rules that scrape all the wealth into their own colossal piles-o-treasure. When the hand curls into an iron fist they pull the legal and economic strings toward the smaller piles-o-treasure and away from their larger ones. Why, in my day I despised inheritance and recommended that it be abolished, or at least severely reduced. Otherwise, indolent father hands down his inherited, undeserved wealth to his indolent, undeserving son![49] But the way they've tied my giant hand today, it destroys thousands of very small savings and accrues ever-more power to the zealous elite that makes the rules, enriching the haves while impoverishing the many hard workers who are just trying to get by. It's an uncouth sight to see. They have my giant hand doing much the opposite of what I intended, and what's worse, they're doing it in my name! I suspect it's your narrow-minded, modern version of economist that's to blame for this travesty. Had they the sense to analyze my works in more depth and detail, they would have seen that I had much reverence for equity, justice, empathy, and generosity. I believed in the inherent equality of people. I think some of your economists have fallen prey to self-deception,

---

of the economy. However, Smith also was a moral philosopher concerned with the socioeconomic abuses of the free market (Fleischacker, 2004; Muller, 1995). While he was a champion of freedom, he most definitely was not, as neoconservative ideologues contend, a proponent of unregulated, selfish greed.

49 Significant estate taxes are paid by only the richest 2% of Americans but conservative pundits and politicians have duped much of the public into thinking that most people suffer from heavy taxation of inheritances. The trickery comes from deceptive terminology such as referring to the estate tax as the "death tax," which makes the levy seem decidedly unfair even though it was implemented in 1916 to ensure that the wealthy few who normally dodged taxation would have to pay their fair share (Graetz & Shapiro, 2005).

which is the cause of much human misery. In order to preserve their flawed pet theories, they've deceived themselves into believing the freedom half of my message while ignoring the equality and justice half. 'Tis something to despair.

Spinner: Now that you're out of the grave, what do you propose to do?

Smith: I don't know laddie, but I will be giving someone a piece of my mind to bring them to a right repentance. Maybe I'll hike over yon hills to those towers, find out who is pulling the big strings, and whack their backsides with my trusty walking stick. Wish me luck laddies. These old knees aren't what they used to be.

Prober: Thank you Mr. Smith. I hope you can enlighten a few string pullers.

Smith brushed 2 centuries of dust from his coat and then limped away toward the lobbyists' control tower. I wondered how much effect a centuries-old, expired Scotsman might have on powerful lobbyists sequestered in a tall, concrete tower. However, their obvious reverence for his name gave me some hope that they would come to appreciate the long-lost moral aspects of his thinking. But then Spinner brought me back to reality.

Spinner: This is a sad day indeed. One of my greatest heroes seems to have lost his mind. Almost everything he said contradicted the Golden Slab. Oh, well, I guess spending a couple of centuries in a grave could give you a severe case of dementia. Let's raise our spirits by driving to Big Boxica, where you'll be able to buy almost anything you want. Nothing like a shopping spree to make you forget your troubles.

―――――――――――― Cн 9. ――――――――――――

BIGGER BOXES IN BIG BOXICA

It was easy to tell when we were within a hundred miles of Big Boxica. The roadsides were so cluttered with advertising billboards that it was difficult to pick out the road signs, or to see around curves. Consequently, a number of traffic accidents made our headway even more difficult. But the wait was worth it. Box Kingdom Supermall, or "the box" as locals called it, was an enormous warehouse-style building 110 feet high, 1/2 mile wide and 2 miles long. Fondly known to Neoconians as the hotbed of consumerism and the center of the materialistic universe, the mall was littered with garish billboards, blinking neon signs, and gigantic corporate logos.[50] The box was said to contain just about every consumer good imaginable. Walking from a sprawling parking lot littered with cardboard, plastic shopping bags, Styrofoam chips, and other assorted trash, and then passing through one of the ornate entrances, we were met by a very old, sallow greeter shuffling behind a walker. She pointed us toward a row of large shopping

―――――

50   In our culture, materialistic consumption has become an end in itself instead of a means to the end of achieving more fundamental self-fulfillment (Mayer, 1998). Our endless pursuit of more and more has distracted us from other possibilities for human enrichment while blinding us to the abuses of corporate monopolies and the excessive concentration of resources in a few hands. In addition, once we have met our basic material needs, pursuit of ever more materialistic wealth has diminishing returns and even undermines our quality of life (Kasser, 2002). Paradoxically, it can make us feel less secure, less connected with others, and less free.

carts where we selected one and made our way onto the moving sidewalk that takes shoppers throughout the facility. I asked Spinner why the greeter wasn't in a retirement home. He told me that she was still working because she was a working-class Near Dreg; they don't retire anymore since the Great Privatization enabled both government and industry to stop paying pensions. As we moved past the storefronts we were bombarded with advertising in various forms—catchy, persistent, repetitive jingles coming from PA systems; signs and stickers emblazoned with corporate slogans and logos; Pundit O. Gasbag on video monitors loudly urging people to shop in the name of patriotism; the image of the Emperor on posters doing the same; hawkers on stilts wearing clown costumes; even small, fettered children wearing corporate logo T-shirts and dancing to product jingles played by organ grinders.

Prober: Can we stop at that clothing store with all the jackets and T-shirts in the window?

Spinner: Sure, this is Affluenza Clothiers. They put corporate logos on all their clothing lines so you can proudly wear the insignia of your favorite corporation.

Prober: Why would you want to do that?

Spinner: Why wouldn't you? All the kids are wearing them, and so are the jocks. I remember the days when sports teams were named after animals, birds, and so forth: the bears, the eagles, and so on. Eventually, the sports franchise owners wised up and made huge profits selling their teams to corporations, which renamed the teams and redesigned the uniforms to advertise themselves. So now the Neoconian Baseball League, the NBL, has teams like the Big Boxica Scrapburgers, named after the fast-food restaurant chain. See that lime green and purple jersey over there with the large burger on it? That's a Scrapburger uniform and it's in hot demand right now. That blood-red shirt over there is the uniform of the Fascisto Assault Rifles, a team owned by Homicidal Industries. Remember them from back in Fascisto? They're the biggest of our nation's 14,000-plus gun manufacturers. And the gold and white jersey with the diamond emblem is the uniform of the White City Bling-Blingers, a team owned by Ostentatious Jewelers. They're famous for those fabulous, four-pound, gold-plated, diamond-studded watches you see the Splendiferous Bluebloods wearing.

Prober: I'm not very athletic so I don't think any of those corporations would want me advertising their team! Can we move on to the electronics store next door?

Spinner: Sure. Among many other gadgets, this place sells a lot of computers. It used to sell the Safeguard K-1000, which parents loved because it set off warning sirens and gave users an electric shock through the keyboard whenever they went to websites that were blacklisted by the Emperor for inappropriate moral or political content. But those computers became obsolete when the Zealot's Court approved the takeover of the Internet by a coalition of the Emperor, Abominate Frenzy, the Dissent Suppression Forum, and Apocalypse Industries.[51] Now the Internet is clean as a whistle and many of the websites carry video clips from Weasel News. Over here are the Mindnumber TV sets, the best on the market. The Mindnumber Vacuous 3000 is the top of the line—160" plasma screen, a 1400-button remote, the works. It even comes with bumper stickers and yard signs saying "I own a Mindnumber Vacuous 3000" so you can show off to the neighbors. Look how clear the shows are on this display set. Just imagine yourself sitting with your mega-remote switching through the 17,000 channels and sampling all the shows. Our entertainment corporations bring you everything imaginable from reality shows to 24-hour shopping ads, to various professional sports, to public executions, to on-the-ground adventure coverage of our wars in the Vassal Lands. Let's flip channels a little and see what we can find now. Here's the reality show "Hungry Hungry Hogs" in which contestants compete with each other to eat the most disgusting things possible. Ha ha, look at that guy scarfing down a pile of raw brains from executed prisoners. Let's see what's on the morality channel. Oh, good, it's the popular cop show, "Run 'Em Down and Snuff 'Em," where our Cleaner Police hunt down shirtless, shoeless Putrid Scum who've had the audacity to escape their designated areas and make their way into exclusive neighborhoods. The show gets really exciting when the cleaners corner one and execute him on the spot using a method voted on by a polling of viewers. Oh, here's another reality show on the rise. It's called "Cheerpower" because teams of cheerleaders in skimpy uniforms compete to make up the best possible corporate cheer. The winner gets to cheer the victorious corporation at the yearly Dodger Awards where the corporations receive their trophies for finding the best loopholes to avoid the few, remaining unfair and oppressive government taxes and regulations. Here's another popular show, "Beat My Bazooms," which is sponsored by the Stupor Drug Company, the makers of the bust-enhancing pill, Elephanesta. It's a game show. The contestants compare bust sizes and then start using Elephanesta. They come back a month later for measurements and the winner gets a year's supply of, guess what—Elephanesta. That show draws a lot of adolescent male viewers.

Prober: What's that infrared beam on the top of the set for? It seems to aim at the viewer.

---

51 Corporate and government interests are attempting to exert considerable control over the Internet (Lovink, 2002)

Spinner: Oh, that's the commercial tracking device; there's a history to it. Long ago, watching TV was free but you had to watch advertisements, which paid for the programming. Then the executives at the Weasel Network thought of ways to increase their profits. One way was to start up cable TV systems so the consumer had to pay monthly fees to watch the shows *and* the ads. Pretty smart, huh. Making consumers pay for the advertisements they were watching doubled the revenue. Of course, one of the best profit maximizers was to increase the length of the ads. When it got to the point where the advertising lasted longer than the shows, people started buying devices that enabled them to fast-forward through the ads. The corporate advertisers didn't like this one bit so they paid their lobbyists to pay the politicians they owned to pass a law that would force the consumer to watch the ads. This was the Compulsory Commercial Gawking Act. It requires every TV sold in the land to have a commercial tracking device that uses an infrared beam to read the retina of the viewer. If a viewer closes his or her eyes or looks away for more than 10 seconds, or switches channels during a commercial, or fast forwards through an advertisement, the device records the infraction and levies an automatic fine of $50, which is transferred from the offender's bank account directly into the account of the corporation running the ad. The law makes everything fair now, and advertisers' profits have skyrocketed. It's one more victory for our free-market system.

Our next stop was the auto dealer complex. Most of the vehicles on display in the dealerships were Excessive Egomobiles, or EEMs for short. Stepping into the showroom of Larceny Motors, we were surrounded by a group of very aggressive salespeople. One of them, a fretful, oily haired, bony fellow whose nametag read Slick N. Desperate, grabbed us by the shirtsleeves and led us over to a monstrous vehicle covered in chrome, lights, and gadgetry.

Slick: Now feast your eyes on this baby. This is our top of the line EEM: the platinum-detailed, jewel-encrusted Earth Devastator. It stands 13 feet high, stretches the length of a school bus, and has all the bells and whistles.[52] Climb up the entry ladder and look inside. There's a 42" plasma TV on the dashboard so you can watch Weasel News or the Scrapburgers' baseball games while you drive. The seat covers are made of extremely rare polar bear hide. You'll certainly impress your friends with that! And look at the back. See that large, 3' X 6' liquid crystal video screen? That's your license plate but you can set it to display your favorite messages. For example, "My son is in Hoity-

---

52 The technological progress we celebrate has taken the hollow, superficial form of flashy bells and whistles with harmful long-term environmental effects. If we were smarter, we would apply our creative tech-savvy minds to the development and production of ecotechnology that would work *with* the environment, not against it (Hughes, 2004).

Toity Château Chic School," or "Dogma University alumnus," or "Support our glorious Emperor," or "Nuke the Vassal Lands."

Prober: A big-screen TV on the dashboard? Shouldn't the driver be paying attention to the road?

Slick: Why should the driver worry? If you hit something in this baby, whatever you hit is gonna lose! That's a big reason people buy these, so they feel safe on the roads.

Prober: It is huge, absolutely enormous. What about gas mileage? It must really suck up the fuel!

Slick: Oh, it gets about 1/2 mile per gallon, which is pretty good for an excessive egomobile vehicle this size. But if you're worried about the cost of fuel you might not be the kind of person who is worthy of driving one of these. I took you for a high-quality kind of guy. I wasn't mistaken, was I?

Prober: Actually, I don't define my worth by what I drive.[53]

Slick: Come on now, you're not some kind of commie are you?

Prober: Just tell me more about the vehicle.

Earth Devastator Excessive Egomobile from Larceny Motors

---

53 We become so distracted by our frenetic quest for ever more material goods that it weakens and distorts our democratic values, turning us from intelligent citizens into mindless consumers (Orlie, 2001).

Slick: Well, these headlights are the brightest on the road—1000 watt high-intensity discharge lamps, and there are 9 of them, four on the right, four on the left, and the big, square one in the middle of the diamond-studded grill. That lamp shines the driver's monogram out ahead to announce his presence on the road. It's so cool; reminds me of the Batman call signal. With all those lights on it seems like high noon even in the middle of the darkest night.

Prober: Aren't the lights too bright? Don't they blind the oncoming drivers?

Slick: Hey, whatever happens to other drivers isn't your concern. If they can't drive safely they shouldn't be on the road.[54] Anyway, the Emperor solved that problem last year. The Larceny Motors lobbyists we own paid him and the senators a lot of money to make a law called the Excessive Egomobile Deference Act, which requires drivers to pull over to the roadside when they see the bright lights of an Earth Devastator coming toward them. That law prevents a lot of accidents I tell you, and it really makes you feel important when you're driving one of these babies. It's like everyone is paying homage to you. Gives you one more reason to buy one. Shall we go into my office and start the paperwork?

Prober: What's that bulge on the top of the vehicle?

Slick: That's the latest thing in excessive egomobile technology: a 360-degree rotating turret cannon for hunting in the wilderness if you take the vehicle off road. It's also helpful for drivers who really get angry on the highway. Of course, the users' manual says to operate it sparingly and with discretion, but this is a free country so that's up to the driver. Everyone knows that Earth Devastators have these cannons, so they're really careful not to cut you off or drive too slowly in front of you. It really cuts down on road rage. And the cannon is easy to use. There's a joystick on the console, just like in a video game. All you do is aim, lock on, and fire. The cannon is a 60 mm rocket launcher with a shaped-charge warhead. For some extra money you can install a sure-shot, heat-seeking rocket so it flies right up the tailpipe or into the radiator of the driver you're aiming at. If that isn't enough, there are other features. See that panel on the roof? It has hidden, pop-up, retractable police lights and a siren to clear the road ahead if you're in a hurry in heavy traffic, just in case the EEM Deference law and your turret cannon don't

---

54 Ricci (2004) argued that consumers must escape their own self-interest enough to exercise their "economic conscience." It is legitimate to pursue self-interest as long as we have conscience enough to realize that our private actions carry consequences for others. For example, the decision to buy a pollution-spewing, gas-guzzling, road-hogging SUV requires at least some awareness that our purchase just created dirtier air, more expensive fuel, and less room for everyone else on already dangerous, crowded roads.

provide sufficient motivation for other drivers to get out of your way. Nobody wants to be stopped by the police. Since the Emperor gave them more power, they've been known to shoot drivers they've pulled over to the roadside to save the trouble of writing a ticket. Of course, the police don't stop these EEMs. They're off limits. One more good reason to buy one.

Prober: Isn't it dangerous to give drivers such powerful weapons?

Slick: Our motto is, turret cannons don't kill people. Drivers kill people. Besides, every responsible citizen carries a gun in Neoconland because the Federal Assault Rifle Confederacy and Homicidal Industries paid their lobbyists to pay their politicians to pass the Compulsory Firearm Totin' law. You may have noticed that all Splendiferous Bluebloods and Insatiable Predators in the land carry weapons everywhere they go, even on the beach. Of course, the Near Dreg and the Putrid Scum classes were exempted from the law because nobody wanted them running around with weapons. They just aren't responsible enough. Anyway, the turret cannons on our Earth Devastators are just bigger guns so they're perfectly legal.[55]

Prober: This is an interesting vehicle. I'll think about it. What others do you have?

Slick: If you can't afford this one, the next step down is the 221 Gold Star Ostentatiousmobile. It's the same excessive egomobile but without a few of the features. Then there's the Vainglorious Enviro-Buster, and if you want to project a really rugged image, you might want to buy the Aggressive Belligerent over there. It's the one with the military camouflage paint, and it doesn't have the polar bear seat covers. But it does have a snowplow blade on the front to scoop unworthy small cars off into the ditch. Does a great job on pokey pedestrians at crosswalks too.

Prober: I don't think I'm ready to purchase yet but I might come back if you give me your card.

Slick: OK, your loss. *[runs off to corner another customer]*.

Prober: Can we go over there on the other side of the mall? See that door marked "Associates Only"?

Spinner: We shouldn't, but you're here to learn everything you can about our wonderful country. Let's go.

---

55 A nation guided by neoconservative ideology must rely heavily on its legal system because it is the primary mechanism for keeping order among large numbers of self-interested, self-aggrandizing, rapaciously materialistic, atomistic individuals. However, a healthy legal system can leave much room for immoral actions because legal rights are not necessarily sound in a moral sense. "Many of us, for example, would say that the legal rights granted to slave-owners over their slaves in the American South before the civil war were legal, but not moral" (Orend, 2002, p. 26).

We passed through the door into a huge, dingy warehouse where some workers were packing, sorting, and piling boxes of merchandize. All the workers were making exactly the same robotic motions at the same time guided by a buzzer attached to a large clock.[56]

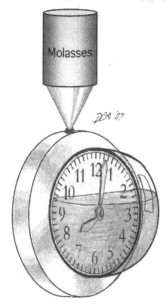

Molasses-Filled Pace Clock

Prober: What's the purpose of the clock?

Spinner: That's the "pace clock." Its buzzer keeps the workers moving in synch and they're very productive. Without it, they would just waste time and chat with each other.

Prober: Why is the clock face partially filled with that gooey brown liquid?

Spinner: That's the molasses. It's a great managerial innovation! You see, the workers are paid 40% of the hourly, minimum wage.[57] A great man by the name of Mountebank Ignominious, the CEO of Box Kingdom Supermall, found a way to make the workers much more productive in order to maximize

56 Big-box shopping outlets create painful irony when their managers get on the PA system and tell associates to clean up the mess in aisle 12. Cleaning up the mess isn't the irony. Calling low-paid, automaton-like workers "associates" is ironic because the designation implies a high level of regard for the worker as colleague. Obviously, the collegial esteem isn't genuine because corporations continue to use exploitative practices to pay their employees as little as possible with minimal benefits (Bakan, 2004) while allowing them little to no workplace autonomy. The term "associates" derives from management gurus who urge businesses to form innovative, semiautonomous work teams that will engage workers' imaginations and intrinsic motivation. It's as though the managers and owners of big-box stores had heard the fancy new terminology but not the underlying message about workplace empowerment. While calling their employees associates, they nevertheless approximate the century-old practice of scientific management, which portrays workers as mindless machines and micromanages their movements to maximize efficiency (Taylor, 1911).

57 Wages in Neoconland always are much less than the "minimum" wage, reflecting the current pressure to suppress or reduce wages in a globalized, unregulated, free-trade economy. In recent decades, the well being of the poorest 20% of Americans stagnated or eroded on every important measure including workplace wages (Massey, 2005).

profits and shareholder dividends while justifying his 38 billion lucre-buck-dollar-a-year compensation package.[58] All it took was a little molasses. See the funnel at the top of the clock? The foreman pours enough molasses into the clock to keep it 2/3 full. The clock hands slow down due to the viscosity of the molasses, so a 14-hour shift, which is the typical workday for a laborer in Neoconland, stretches out to 19 hours on your watch. That's nearly a 36% productivity increase![59] The business world is captivated by Mr. Ignominious and his ideas. His recent book, *Managing with Molasses and Other Great Ideas,* is near the top of the bestseller list, and he's a regular interview on the Pundit O. Gasbag show.

Before leaving the mall, Spinner slipped into a Weasel News Trifle and Doohickey Shop to pick up a Pundit O. Gasbag Super-Media Hero action figure as a gift for his nephew's 27ʰ birthday. Later, back out in the parking lot, we passed a Stupor Drugs store.

---

58   Green (2005) reported contrasting economic trends in developed nations over the past few decades. While average pay levels have increased, with the notable exception of the United States, and many jobs have been created, job quality has diminished considerably. Employees have less influence and autonomy, their job satisfaction has eroded, and the level of effort expected by employers has risen dramatically. Much of this has occurred because labor unions have been diminishing in power and disintegrating (Fairbrother & Griffin, 2002) largely due to attacks by prominent, early neoconservatives such as Margaret Thatcher and Ronald Reagan. Adding to the injustice, the average compensation of corporate chief executive officers expanded enormously, from 42 times the pay of an average worker in 1980 to a ratio of 280 to 1 in 2004, and the gap continues to widen unchecked (Bogle, 2005).

59   The pace clock symbolizes the rampant exploitation of working people in a world dominated by neoclassical economic globalization. The exploitation takes various forms ranging from the destruction of unions to the serious erosion of workplace regulations, to the proliferation of dangerous, draconian sweatshops approximating slavery, to downright actual slavery. The new forms of globalized slavery trap over 27 million people in forced labor (Bales, 1999). Moreover, the new slavery is even harsher than the old in one important sense. In the past, slaves were long-term investments so it benefited the slave owners to look after at least the basic, physical needs of their human property. But today's slaves are cheap, disposable, and easy to replace with other desperate people, making it easier for owners to abuse, starve, and discard them. Discussing another form of exploitation, Perrow (2002) argued that private corporations are dominated by large, bureaucratic organizational systems that undermine individual freedom. The irony is that corporate-friendly neoconservatives harshly criticize big government for establishing similar large, freedom-eroding bureaucracies.

Prober: While you were in the checkout line buying your doll I stepped outside near this drugstore and bumped into some people who really seem to need welfare. They looked desperate.

Spinner: Yeah, they really need welfare. Without it, I don't think they would last very long in this world.

Prober: They do look like they don't have two nickels to rub together. That old woman over there in the ragged dress told me she's a nurse who lost her job in the latest round of downsizings. She said that now the nursing in the hospitals is done by videoconference from India.[60] Seems like poor bedside manner to me. And her friend is a retired teacher. They were picking through the trashcans looking for lunch when I ran into them.

Spinner: You're looking at the decrepit shoppers over there? You think they need welfare?! No, I mean the owners and financiers of Stupor Drugs, the big pharmaceutical corporation. We have to give *them* corporate welfare so they can think up new drugs and get them on the market. We call it corporate welfare because investing in the very best people makes the whole nation fare well.

Prober: Correct me if I'm wrong but I heard on the boat trip over here that the government scientists invent the drugs and the pharmaceutical corporations just capitalize on the discoveries.

Spinner: Well, yes, the scientists rely on taxpayer money to support their research and then the production people from Stupor Drugs take the patents that come from the research and mass-produce the new drugs.[61] But if we told Stupor Drugs how to use their corporate welfare grants it would intrude on their freedom and the invisible hand of the market wouldn't like that one bit. They really invest most of their research and development money in marketing, which is a form of inventing or research and development when you think about it. And marketing brings in even more money so they can keep the industry growing. It all works out in the end.

An armored car pulled up to the front door of the drugstore.

Prober: They must be here to take away some of those profits.

---

60 Outsourcing of work to foreign sweatshops is a growing problem in an increasingly unregulated, global economy (Applebaum, 2005).

61 Goozner (2005) revealed some troubling dynamics of the highly profitable pharmaceutical industry, which justifies the high cost of drugs by claiming high research and development costs. Actually, university and government laboratories do most of the R & D so taxpayers are paying twice for enormously expensive drugs: first by footing the bill for university and government pharmaceutical research and second by purchasing the expensive drugs from pharmaceutical corporations. In short, the high cost of drugs emerges not from R & D costs but from deceptive corporate profiteering.

Spinner: No, they're not here to get cash. They're dropping off pills. Since the Great Deregulation of the Great Privatization deregulated the drug industry, the pills became more valuable. Stupor Drugs transports them in armored cars because the average single pill costs $700. Wish I had Stupor stock. Those pills are worth much more than gold now.[62]

Prober: I assume the Great Deregulation loosened government oversight of industry?

Spinner: Oh yes! This was one of the greatest accomplishments in world history. Before the Great Privatization brought forth the Great Deregulation, business and industry had to spend time and effort being careful about the safety of their products and the honesty of their advertising. That was a real drag on productivity. With the Great Deregulation all government agencies that regulated business and industry shut down and corporations were asked to monitor themselves on the honor system.[63] With the combination of the Great Deregulation and the Corporate Protection Act, which outlawed lawsuits and criticism of our wonderful corporations, our economy burst wide open and our biggest investors made barrels of lucre-buck dollars!

Still out in the parking lot, turning away from Stupor Drugs, I noticed a gargantuan store right next door.

Prober: That's the biggest pet food store I've ever seen!

Spinner: The Splendiferous Bluebloods and many of the Insatiable Predators do love their poodles. You'll often find their servants in here buying the upscale dog food, the really good stuff. You may have seen their products advertised on Weasel TV. They sell a wide variety of dog food including hand-wrapped portions of Hummingbird Brain, Truffle Studded Sea Bass, Pompous Poopsy Caviar, and Shark Fin Nibbles, among others.

Prober: I see that the upscale section is only a small part of the store. What's in all the rest?

Spinner: That's the bulk dog food. It's made of animal fat, entrails, scraps of hide, hooves, sawdust, and other such things. Most people buy it for their

---

62 According to a recent study carried out by Harvard Medical School researchers, the privatized American medical system costs about twice as much per capita and provides much less in comparison with Canada's public system (Lasser, Himmelstein, & Woolhandler, 2006). Americans are much more likely to forego needed medicines due to cost, and much less likely to have access to a regular doctor. Consequently, American's are more likely to suffer from chronic diseases while Canadians are healthier and enjoy longer life spans.

63 The Bush administration clamped down on government regulatory initiatives. For example, by stonewalling the enforcement of environmental laws, they relieved polluters of responsibility for the damage they were causing (see Hacker & Pierson, 2005).

pets. And most members of the Putrid Scum class do their grocery shopping here, as long as they haven't frittered away their money on booze, drugs, gambling, and who knows what else.

Prober: Did you just say grocery shopping?!

Spinner: Yes, they can't afford to shop at the regular markets. But the dog food is a good option for them. It has protein. The dogs you've seen are healthy, aren't they? Since the Great Privatization eliminated government and corporate pensions, most senior citizens also shop here. Putting these two stores side by side was a stroke of genius on the part of Mountebank Ignominious, the CEO of the Supermall. Now the seniors can one-stop shop for their pills and groceries. Well, better turn in for the night. Got us rooms in that five-star hotel across the street. Have a good rest because it's a long trip to White City and Toxica tomorrow. You're in for a change because we'll be taking the train there. But don't worry about having to rub elbows with any Near Dregs or Putrid Scum. I got us first-class tickets. See you in the morning.

—————— Сн 10. ——————

STARTLING CONTRASTS BETWEEN
WHITE CITY AND TOXICA

After a long but interesting train ride through the Neoconland interior passing by enormous factory farms, tumbledown shells of abandoned family farmhouses, and some gaping strip mines, we finally headed down into Empathy Gulf Valley[64] where Flaming Filth River separates two large cities: White City on the plateau overlooking the west bank of the river and Toxica, a huge slum city in the swampland on the east bank. For a couple of hours our arrival was presaged by an increasingly oppressive browning of the air, which became chokingly rank as we neared the outskirts of Toxica. At the bottom of the valley, our train ran along the eastern riverfront on the Toxica side where we could see large meatpacking plants, tanneries, and the enormous oil refinery run by Coughing Coal-Black Industries. Large pipes running from these plants to the riverbank were pouring

———————

64   The valley is named for the empathy gulf phenomenon articulated by Shapiro (2003). Arguing that a primary purpose of democratic governance is to prevent domination, Shapiro warned that large power differentials such as extreme wealth disparities can generate empathy gulfs, which are chasms of understanding between haves and have nots. The haves develop an empathy-eroding psychological distance from their unfortunate peers who live in vastly different neighborhoods and travel in different circles. Meanwhile, those who live on the deprived side of the empathy gulf develop resentment, deviant behavior, and even attitudes favorable to revolution.

thousands of gallons of slimy effluent directly into the river. The water was a rusty brown viscous syrup with large clumps of rotting matter floating on top. Some of these clumps were on fire, hence the name Flaming Filth River.[65] *Bloated parts of animal carcasses floated by, along with the occasional human corpse.*[66] *On land, run-down, crowded, tarpaper and corrugated-tin shacks pressed right up against the factory fences and spread away to the east past the horizon. Looking the other way across the river through the smog we could just make out White City's gleaming high-rise towers and spacious, pristine parks.*

Prober: Why does White City look so nice while Toxica is a huge slum?

Spinner: It just worked out that way. The people in White City own and operate the industrial plants. The executives ride across Segregation Bridge[67] in their limos to work in the offices at the top of the plants. Look up there at the top of the office complex attached to the Coughing Coal-Black refinery. See those huge windows facing White City? That's where their executives work. Their estates are over in the gated communities across the river. So are the homes of the shareholders and their families.

---

65 The chemically contaminated Cuyahoga River in Cleveland, Ohio, actually caught fire during a time of weak environmental regulation because it was used as a dumpsite for industrial facilities (Shiva, 2002). Our economic system tends to ignore the costs of environmental damage, sloughing it off as a burden for the general public; hence, corporate operations should pay the unrecognized environmental costs they generate instead of getting an environmental free ride at public expense (Hawken, 1993).

66 Environmental racism is putting the health of millions at risk (Bullard, 2005; Pellow, 2002). Lax enforcement and corrupt evasion of already weak environmental protection regulations represent a form of human-rights abuse because toxic industrial facilities are placed in impoverished areas where the residents lack the political power to resist. This problem persists within America and between nations. In America, the result is the creation of toxic, sacrifice zones such as "Cancer Alley" in Louisiana where numerous polluting industrial facilities are located. Internationally, affluent nations export their toxic trash to poor regions in underdeveloped nations (Pellow, 2007). Studying other aspects of the differences that separate populations, Massey and Denton (1998) described the persistence of racial and class segregation in America, which has taken the form of hypersegregation: an all-pervasive intensified form of ghettoization created by whites. When those living in the ghetto adapt to their harsh circumstances they develop dispositions and behavioral patterns that magnify their differences with mainstream culture even more, thereby reinforcing the segregation they suffer.

67 A dynamic tension exists between community and individualism in America (Kirp, 2000). The latter, which is at the core of neoconservative ideology, makes it easier for us to establish and maintain the barriers of racial and class segregation, thereby locking some children into low-opportunity ghettos.

Prober: Who lives over here in Toxica?

Spinner: The workers in the plants and refineries of course. Actually, many of the people in Toxica came from the rural areas when they went bankrupt and lost their farms. Many more came from towns where the businesses outsourced their work offshore to sweatshops in the foreign Vassal Lands. They came here looking for work. The few lucky ones got jobs, and they really were lucky because they make almost 50% of minimum wage. The rest of them crowd around the plants every morning hoping to land work for the day.[68] The plants don't hire workers to long-term positions. They make them compete every minute of every hour and they fire at least the slowest 60% of them every day. That way, the hungriest, most desperate workers keep working very hard, which is good for them, and the plants keep their workers highly motivated.[69] As always, our system is a win-win for everyone.

---

68 Government policy currently reflects neoconservative assumptions that the poor can escape their miserable conditions through their own efforts if only they would stop being lazy and try a little harder. While there always will be individual cases in which this is true, scholars are concluding that notions of autonomous, individual self-determination and the deprived escaping poverty through individual effort alone are flawed (see Ambrose, 2002, 2003, 2005, 2009; Bowles, Durlauf, & Hoff, 2006; Fischer et al., 1996; Laird, 2006; MacLeod, 1994; Wuthnow, 2006). Instead, the setting into which children are born can trap them within desperate conditions making escape from poverty a long shot. The mythology that frames and promotes our reverence for individualism, such as the Horatio Alger myth of the poor pulling themselves up by their bootstraps, actually works to prevent us from creating a more just and equitable society (Wuthnow). Laird showed how access to the inner social networking circles of the privileged plays a crucial part in determining who is successful in today's business environment. Networking connections with the powerful are huge advantages in the competitive marketplace and the deprived simply don't have access to them. In addition, deprivation, stigmatization, and segregation pose daunting barriers to the development of aspirations among the impoverished (Ambrose; Fischer et al.; MacLeod). Strong aspirations (motivating life goals) are essential to the development of talents and the pursuit of self-fulfillment. Lacking access to influential support networks and other key resources, and lacking opportunities to develop strong aspirations, even highly intelligent and talented young impoverished people have little chance for lofty accomplishment in a decidedly inegalitarian society.

69 "Flexible management systems" enable employers to hire, fire, and "bench" workers who serve volatile, project-based markets and such markets are becoming more prevalent in the globalized economy. Xiang (2007) analyzed the dynamics of one such system: the highly volatile and flexible body-shopping of information-technology workers from India. Consultants recruit the workers who are shifted around from one worksite to another and perfunctorily benched

But even more jobs come open. Many vacancies occur because the workers are so stupid and clumsy that quite a few of them are maimed or killed every day in workplace accidents. There weren't nearly as many job openings in the old days before the Great Deregulation got rid of workplace safety rules. You don't want to spend much time on this side of the river. There's a lot of theft, vandalism, starvation, disease, murder, you name it. The people here are vile, just vile! Anyway, I hope the train soon turns westward toward White City.

Prober: Those plants must hire a lot of workers but there can't possibly be room for all the people of working age in Toxica. The slum is so huge. There must be many millions here.

Spinner: You said working age. There is no working age since we eliminated child labor laws in the Great Deregulation. Now everyone has the opportunity to work, even toddlers if they can find something they're capable of doing.[70] But you're right about the unemployment. Probably 80% of the people in Toxica can't get work because there are just too many of them. Most spend their days picking through Trash Mountain over there looking for useful pieces of garbage they can eat, barter, or sell.[71]

(i.e., laid off) for indeterminate lengths of time after the completion of specific projects. Under the body shopping system, employers have the benefit of extreme labor flexibility while the workers have little or no stability or security. Such uncertainty generates social and emotional trauma for individuals and societies (Sennett, 2005).

70 Child labor is a big part of labor exploitation in today's globalized world (see Bales, 1999).

71 Currie (2006) showed that the American social safety net may be full of holes but it still provides important services saving many poor families from even greater destitution in times of misfortune. Unfortunately, this minimal safety net is under attack and in danger of further shredding. Welfare reform is hailed as a great success because it significantly reduced the welfare rolls. But research into the life experiences of former welfare recipients showed that this success came at the expense of considerable human misery (see Hays, 2004). Over 90% of recipients were impoverished single mothers. Welfare reform forced them to juggle difficult child-rearing responsibilities with dead-end, menial work with no benefits. They couldn't afford the childcare needed to free them for work commitments and affordable transportation to and from work typically was not available in a nation that doesn't invest in public transit. Ironically, welfare reform was promoted by neoconservative ideologues who expressed great enthusiasm for family values while forcing working mothers to work for basic survival while leaving their children home alone or on the streets. The exploitation of women workers as a low-pay reserve labor force (Kessler-Harris, 2003) and a shock absorber for the economy further aggravates the problem. In addition, our neoconservative-dominated socioeconomic system has promoted the

75

Starving Child on Toxica's Trash Mountain

Prober: That mountain is made of trash? I thought it was a real mountain because you can see it for miles. How did it get so big?

Spinner: The Happyrefuse Company created this as a depository for most of the garbage in the region. When we go over to White City you'll notice that there's no garbage of any kind anywhere. What you will see are trash-picking teams of day laborers from Toxica and chain gangs from the prison picking up every piece of rubbish all the way down to the smallest toothpick and then dumping it in gleaming white tanks that are hauled away in the evening by Happyrefuse trucks. All of the garbage goes to this trash mountain in Toxica. A large part of Trash Mountain also comes from the industrial plants. The slaughterhouses dump the lowest grade animal entrails and bones up there,

demonization of children with punitive policies such as three-strikes legislation and the proliferation of disciplinary boot camps. Meanwhile, other developed nations, which are much less influenced by neoconservative ideology, provide more widespread social support for early child development (Lubeck, 1995).

you know, the diseased stuff that isn't good enough to put in dog food. The refineries dump broken machine parts, barrels of grease, and so on.

Prober: The White City trash trucking seems inefficient. Why don't they just make a trash pile over on the White City side so they don't have to travel far?

Spinner: They would never allow that in White City! It would lower the property values. Besides, dumping the trash over here gives the unemployed Toxicans something to do. If it weren't for Trash Mountain, many of them would starve.[72]

Peering high up the side of Trash Mountain through my binoculars, I could see thousands of grimy, skeletal figures slogging and stumbling knee-deep through vermin-infested muck, picking through the rotting trash.[73] Some were lying down in the muck, either dozing off or dying. It was hard to tell which. At the base of the mountain, little children were trying to sell a wide assortment of refuse from old bottle caps, to broken clock radios, to discarded toothbrushes. Near my train window, I saw a small girl trying to trade a slimy watermelon rind for a festering piece of fly-covered animal fat.[74] Fortunately, the train turned and went

---

72 As desperate as things are on Trash Mountain, there is hope for the alleviation of desperate poverty. One promising example comes from the work of Muhammad Yunus (2003), the "banker to the poor" who recently won a Nobel Peace Prize for his innovative microcredit system though which small loans are made to poor people who have no collateral. Most beneficiaries of his system are poor women with no other options. Microcredit has been a great success lifting millions out of poverty. While making huge, positive differences for the individuals involved, microcredit also can alleviate social ills such as the unrest and violence that tend to arise from sustained, widespread, hopeless poverty.

73 A prominent historian (Davis, 2006) described the explosive growth of desperate slums, which provide miserable homes to over a billion people worldwide. These slums are disconnected from the world economy so the residents represent a large discarded segment of humanity with few or no prospects for decent lives. One aspect of the phenomenon is the emergence of garbage hills that support trash picking and bartering in underground economies. The growth of these slums arises from flaws in our globalized economy, which energetically transfers ever more power and resources from the poor to the wealthy throughout the world.

74 Perceptions of the reasons for poverty have changed over time (Katz, 1997; O'Connor, 2001). In the progressive era of the early 20th century many analysts believed poverty came from the socioeconomic and political pressures on the individual: pressures such as exploitation of workers, high unemployment, and low wages. From this viewpoint, the individual bears little responsibility for his or her economic misfortune. In recent decades, during the ascendance of the neoconservatives, the assumptions have shifted to emphasize personal

toward Segregation Bridge and White City. At the entrance to the bridge we saw a barricaded, razor-wired checkpoint with armed guards wearing camouflage uniforms and carrying assault rifles. A long line of bedraggled wretches wearing maids' uniforms and gardeners' overalls were being questioned and searched as they approached the checkpoint.

Spinner: What's going on here?

Prober: Those are the domestics who live in Toxica but work on the estates of White City. They have to be checked here to make sure no undesirables come across to the west bank where they don't belong. They also strip search them going back home the other way at night to make sure they didn't steal anything from their employers.

Once across the bridge, the train turned up into the rolling hills of White City where the upscale, high-rise luxury condos and suburban communities were found. The city contained many gated subdivisions, each of which boasted a set of large concrete McMansions with Plexiglas windows, uniform floor plans, and identical ornate facades. Arriving at Cowboy Clod train station, we were met by a nattily uniformed attendant who loaded us into an iridescent orange Earth Devastator for a tour of the city. We were to visit the Merit family, one of the most prominent Splendiferous Blueblood families in the nation. We started out of the station parking lot onto the 16-lane thoroughfare heading toward the most exclusive suburbs of White City.

Prober: Why is the station named Cowboy Clod?

---

responsibility while removing blame from society. In fact, Margaret Thatcher, the prominent, neoconservative, former Prime Minister of Britain went so far as to make the imbecilic claim that there is no such thing as society (Rapley, 2004). Now, the individual is assumed to be entirely at fault if he or she is poor. Dismantling of programs that support the poor occurs when such assumptions prevail. In Neoconland, the garbage pickers on Trash Mountain are assumed to be entirely to blame for their plight and any efforts to help them would be foolish. This seems particularly disingenuous because the only blame neoconservatives can level at poor children is their unwise "choice" of birth into impoverished families. Poverty severely limits the opportunities children will have in the future (Duncan, Yaung, Brooks-Gunn, & Smith, 1998). In the last three decades, child poverty in developed nations has remained stable with the exception of the United Kingdom and the United States where it has increased markedly (Rainwater & Smeeding, 2003). These two nations are more strongly influenced by neoconservative ideology than other developed nations. Individual rights and freedom of choice are necessary but insufficient bases for democracy (Sandel, 2005). According to Habermas (1996) the right to a decent standard of living is the basis for all other democratic rights such as legal protection and individual liberty. Without this base-line right, a democracy is hollow and tenuous at best.

Spinner: Haven't you heard of Cowboy Clod? He was our first real Emperor. Originally an actor, he played in a lot of B movies so he came to believe that he really was a cowboy gunfighter, even when they turned off the studio lights and he left the set for the night. When he retired he still thought he was a cowboy and the people really seemed to like it. So some clever fellows from the Glorious Birthright Foundation think tank recruited him to run for president. "President" was the name of the head of the federal government before they tore up the old constitution, discovered the Golden Slab, and created the Emperorship. Anyway, Cowboy Clod was such a great Emperor that they named a lot of things after him including this rail station. Since he thought he really was a cowboy gunslinger he started a lot of wars and made the rest of the world fear us, as they should. He also presided over the Great Privatization. He would go on Weasel News TV shows and pull out his six guns blasting away at cardboard cutout dolls representing the evil workers' unions. The people loved it. The Great Privatization wasn't really his idea though. Actually, truth be told, he wasn't bright enough to think up most of the things that happened during his Emperorship. But he was charismatic and could spout off empty platitudes with pizzazz so the lobbyists were able to pull his strings from behind the scenes and get most of their ideas implemented. It was a wonderful time in our nation's history.

Passing by more gleaming condo towers and gated communities, we headed up into the hills where the Merits lived among the most exclusive estates.

Prober: These are very impressive homes but I notice that they're all made of concrete. Why is that?

Spinner: They had to start using reinforced concrete when the hurricanes and tornadoes from global warming became too intense. Even the best homes in this part of the country were being torn apart by record winds way over the top end of the Beaufort wind force scale. All of these homes now are perfectly safe. In addition to the concrete walls they have thick, bulletproof windows, backup generators, pumps to keep floodwaters away, and scrubbers to clean the toxic air. Oh, here we are at the Merit estate.

Two burly armed guards opened the ornate wrought-iron gates and we headed up the broad, tree-lined, cobblestone driveway toward the manor house, which sat majestically at the top of the hill a mile away. The mansion was a classic of Gothic architecture with huge, ornamented windows, towers, and flying buttresses. As we approached the manor we saw several hundred immaculately dressed servants standing at attention on the expansive lawn. Most were wearing gas masks for protection against the acrid air of the Toxica-White City region.

Spinner: Nice place, eh? It has over 700 rooms, including the great hall where the Merits entertain their friends from government and industry. They

Cowboy Clod: The First Emperor

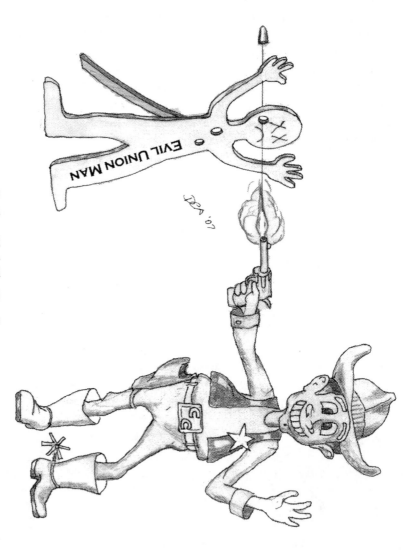

even have an Olympic size swimming pool in the middle of the hall to make their fishman visitors from the think tanks more comfortable.

As we climbed down the ladder from the Earth Devastator a distinguished old gentleman in a flawless tuxedo greeted us and announced himself as the butler. He led us through the massive oak doors into the foyer and then into the palatial grand hall where he introduced us to the current master of the manor.

Butler: Mr. Merit sir, these are the visitors you were expecting: Mr. Prober, the reporter from the foreign land, and Mr. Spinner, his guide from the National Propaganda Ministry. Gentlemen, you are indeed privileged. Meet Mr. Unearnest Merit III Esquire, the exalted lord of Merit Manor and the latest in a long line of esteemed Merits. Mr. Merit's great uncle was Miserly Merit III, the famous minister of finance in the nation's early years. His cousin was Mercenary Merit, the secretary of Aggression in the Cowboy Clod administration. And his great grandfather was Crony Nepotist Merit, the first president of Stupor Drugs Pharmaceutical Corporation.

Prober: Very pleased to meet you sir.

Unearnest: Likewise I'm sure.

Spinner: Mr. Merit, would you please give us a little background about yourself so our guest will understand what separates people like you from the rest of the population?

Unearnest Merit III Esquire: Exalted Lord of Merit Manor

Unearnest: Certainly. As you can see, I come from the best stock. My family has owned much of the land in White City and several factories over in Toxica for generations. I grew up here on the estate and went to Hoity-Toity Château Chic School where I finished in the top 80% of my graduating class. After secondary school I toured the world for a few years. I liked Bora Bora the best. I think it's in Russia, or maybe Iceland? Upon returning home at age 21 I enrolled in the Dogma University business school, which is housed in prestigious Merit Hall, the centerpiece of the campus and my daddy's gift to the university. At age 34 I graduated with my Bachelor's degree in creative accounting[75] and then immediately enrolled in the Masters in Business Admiration program. I graduated with my MBA at age 43 and now I run the tanning factory my daddy gave me for my 46th birthday.

Prober: Very impressive. Was it difficult getting your MBA?

Unearnest: Not at all. I passed everything with flying colors. By the way, if you ever hear anyone saying that my private tutors attended classes for me and wrote my exams, don't you believe it.

Prober: How do you handle things at the tanning factory? Are you a hands-on manager?

Unearnest: Well, I guess you might say I'm quite hands off. I don't go over there to the factory because I think the city of Toxica is disgusting. I delegate everything to Odious Thrash, an old classmate from Dogma University. He's a great motivator and he keeps me informed by e-mail and videoconference. But running the factory is just a hobby for me anyway. I make most of my money by investing the inheritance my daddy gave me. Not that I need to make any more money.

Prober: How do you do your investing? Can you describe your stock portfolio?

Unearnest: Oh, I can't be bothered with silly details. My accountants and brokers do all that... They give me a report on my earnings every few months and that keeps me up to speed. But enough about me. Let's have a look around the great hall. See those portraits of me, my daddy, my uncle, my grandfather, and the other important Merits? Each one was done by the greatest artist of the era. There are copies hanging in most of the hallways of

---

75 Unearnest Merit may not be smart enough to initiate his own corrupt, creative accounting but the financial professionals he mindlessly hires certainly are. Large numbers of wealthy individuals and corporations now engage in unprecedented levels of income-tax cheating (Barlett & Steele, 2002). Neoconservatives within and beyond Congress have been undermining and manipulating the IRS to reduce tax rates and regulations on the affluent while shifting the burden to everyone else. Corrupt executives at lawless, Enron-like corporations are leading the way in this initiative.

the most famous buildings at Dogma University, in Lobbyville, and in the Rotunda of Government House. Over on this wall you can see my honorary degrees from Dogma University. There's my honorary duck-you-rates—oops! I mean doctorates. They gave me my first one of those when my daddy cut them a check for a few hundred million. Oh, look at the time! I'm sorry; we'll have to stop this short. I'm late for my daily massage and manu... mano...manicure! That's the word. Notice that I'm always learning, growing my vocib...vocub...vocabulary! One of my personal assistants is giving me a word a day to keep me mentally sharp. Today's word is manicure. Yesterday's was vocabulary. The day before was justice. I really had trouble with that one. Anyway, nice meeting you and enjoy the rest of your trip.

We stepped back outside onto the spacious, manicured lawn.

Spinner: Interesting fellow, isn't he?

Prober: That's for sure. He's nothing like what I expected. But given his pedigree, his MBA, and his leadership of a major corporation, wouldn't you think he should be able to handle rather simple vocabulary like that?[76]

---

76 The eminent economist John Kenneth Galbraith scoffed at common assumptions that wealthy people such as Unearnest Merit III Esquire must be smart. While some obviously are intelligent, others certainly are not. Galbraith (1996) put it succinctly: "Nothing in modern attitudes is believed more to signify exceptional intelligence than association with large pools of money. Only immediate experience with those so situated denies the myth" (pp. 37-38). Aside from the obvious benefits of prestige, these assumptions of monetarily magnified intelligence also bring the affluent tangible rewards. For example, bankers scrutinize the borrowing of modest loans on the assumption that the borrowers must not be intelligent whereas borrowers of large sums receive little scrutiny because they are assumed to be highly intelligent (Galbraith, 1997). Scholars use the term "unearned merit" as a designation for affluent people such as Unearnest Merit III Esq. who do little or nothing to earn their high status in life (see Davis & Meyer, 2000). According to Phillips (2002), wealth creation in recent decades has shifted from earned income such as salaries to unearned income such as investments and inheritances. Capitalist nations protect unearned merit through unfair inheritance laws favoring the indolent (Webb & Webb, 1995). Recent, massive cuts to the estate tax, which benefit only the wealthiest of Americans, magnify unearned merit even further (Graetz & Shapiro, 2005). Wealth accumulation always has derived primarily from unearned income, especially in the most unequal developed nations. For example, by the turn of the 21st century in the United States "some 15,000 to 25,000 heirs constituted the mainstays of what was quietly becoming an American hereditary aristocracy. Had the United States had a British-type peerage, dozens in the fourth or fifth generation of descent would have been second earls or third viscounts" (Phillips, 2002, p. 118).

Spinner: You can't argue with success. If he wasn't smart he wouldn't be where he is today. Besides, he seems a lot smarter than the great newsman Pundit O. Gasbag and you saw how successful he is. Facts are facts and success is success. Speaking of smart, it's time to visit the National Science Institute where our prize-winning scientists do their cutting-edge work. I had a driver bring my SUV to the estate and here he is coming up the driveway. Let's go see some scientists.

Ch 11.

Monkeymen and Great Inventions at the National Science Institute

Hidden away in a well-treed suburban valley, the National Science Institute certainly was an interesting mix of old and new. The new wing of the building was a gleaming steel and glass addition that contrasted vividly with the much smaller, dilapidated, original structure. The old wing showed evidence of a vibrant past, which was now long gone as revealed by the disintegration of its once flamboyant façade. Its section of the parking lot was nearly empty and overgrown with weeds while the parking lot for the new addition was well maintained and full of spanking new excessive egomobile vehicles. Heading into the old wing of the institute, we opened the rusty, creaking main door and walked down a musty hallway littered with empty boxes, moldering trash, and skittering vermin. As we approached the end of the hallway, we could hear a din coming from behind a door labeled "National Department of Basic Science Stuff and Miscellaneous Whatnots." Stepping through the doorway, Spinner warned me to watch for flying debris, and to avoid any sudden moves. Inside the large science lab, several tired, old, grumpy scientists in dirty lab coats were working on experiments, measuring chemical solutions in beakers, heating liquids over Bunsen burners, checking gauges, and peering through microscopes. Oddly, three agitated, stooped over ape-like men, also dressed in lab coats, were hooting, screeching, and clambering over the experimental equipment, knocking over beakers, breaking vials, spilling chemicals, and periodically flinging dung at the scientists.

Spinner: Since the neocons took over the government, they've changed the regulatory process to ensure that science "does good stuff" while promoting morality. While deregulating business and industry they applied much more stringent regulation to the work of scientists, for the betterment of our utopian nation.

Prober: What's with the monkeymen?

Spinner: Interesting fellows, aren't they? As I understand it, they're the results of genetic engineering experiments gone awry. Our most innovative genetic engineering company, MutantGene Inc., wanted to make clones of our first Emperor so exact replicas of Cowboy Clod could be appointed as leaders of puppet regimes in foreign nations when we conquered them, but for some reason these monkeymen were the result. Fortunately, they inherited the Emperors' love of moral absolutes and other family values as well as the free market of course, so they make excellent overseers of the scientific research in this lab.

Hear No Warnings: Apeman Regulator of Scientific Research

Prober: They don't look very bright. How do they carry out their supervision?

Spinner: Yes, they are quite dull-witted, dumb as three bags of hammers actually, but that's good because they stay focused on their jobs—no worrying about ethics, shades of gray, or anything frivolous like that. The current Emperor assigned these monkeymen to oversee the scientists who couldn't be trusted to do good science because they were trained in the old universities before those cruddy, old institutions were replaced by Dogma University in the Great Privatization.[77] Believe it or not those old universities actually taught useless things like ethics and critical thinking and they failed to follow the Golden Slab, hence the takeover.

Prober: But I still don't get how the monkeymen supervise the work of scientists.

Spinner: When the monkeymen see the scientists are up to something that threatens either corporate interests or public morality, they chastise them by screeching, tipping over and breaking lab equipment, and by flinging ideological dung at them.[78] Just watch. Over there at the biology table, see

---

77 The primary purposes of universities include the pursuit and dissemination of knowledge but predatory capitalism is changing the purposes and dynamics of higher learning (Slaughter & Leslie, 1997). Government support for university teaching and research has been eroding so universities are becoming more entrepreneurial and market-oriented. Faculty scholars are transforming into prole-like "employees" and knowledge is becoming a "commodity." Academic disciplines of the most value to industry (e.g., science, technology, business programs) are gaining support while those with strong contributions to the development of mind but with less obvious monetary payback value are being marginalized (e.g., libraries, social sciences, humanities). The integrity of research and knowledge creation is at stake.

78 The Bush administration persistently filled administrative positions and scientific-review panels with ideological cronies in efforts to warp scientific research findings to suit their policies (Herrera, 2004; Shulman, 2007). The goals were to appease industrial interests by freeing them from government regulation and to align science with conservative moral positions on issues such as stem-cell research. Along with other industries, drug and chemical companies themselves have worked to distort scientific findings by manufacturing artificial uncertainty about otherwise clear research discoveries (Michaels, 2005). Such intellectual suppression by government and industry bears watching because punishing intellectuals and suppressing their work always has been a hallmark of totalitarian regimes. For example, intellectuals were persecuted brutally during the genocidal reign of Cambodia's radical communist Pol Pot regime. Only 300 of 380,000 artists and intellectuals survived that horrific purge (Jacobson, 1997). While the Neoconservative manipulation of science is far from that extreme, it

the monkeyman with the blindfold? His name is See No Progress because he smashes any experiments that smell evil according to his admirable, moral sensibilities. Due to the blindfold, he stumbles around blindly when he's upset about the bad science he smells but he always finds his target, and then he goes wild—very impressive indeed! Right now he's breaking up a stem-cell experiment. He's blindfolded because seeing the big picture might interfere with his super-sensitive political sniffer.

The one over there with the big earplugs is named Hear No Warnings. He goes berserk whenever a scientist tries to imply that our wonderful corporations are harming us in some way. For example, see that bedraggled old scientist sitting on the floor in the corner? She's been sobbing for several days because Hear No Warnings smashed all of her climate gauges and started tearing out some of her hair after she removed one of his earplugs and whispered a caution about global warming. He's been screeching, swinging on the light fixtures, and flinging dung ever since.

And that third one over there; his name is Speak No Sense. He's the only monkeyman with the ability to speak because he was dunked in the Superficial Surface Skimming think tank for a few years. If you listen to him, you'll realize that he's quite articulate, even sounding elegant at times. But he always has that wild-eyed look about him, and he's even better than his brothers at flinging ideological dung. He was appointed to replace the Environmental Protection Agency administrator, the fool who had been trying to get Coughing Coal-Black Industries to install scrubbers in their smokestacks to keep mercury poisoning under control. He's quite a worker, too. After a long day of harassing the scientists, he's always willing to go out into the parking lot and speak with a Weasel News crew about the latest scientific issue. He seems to have a thing for Britney Bubblehead, the perky, buxom Weasel News investigative reporter you might have seen on TV here.

Prober: Can I ask you about the crying scientist who warned about global warming? When we were visiting the think tanks you argued that global warming doesn't exist, but that isn't the consensus of the scientists around the world. They warn about rising sea levels, severe flooding in some places, devastating droughts in others, starvation, violent storms, and the spread of disease, among other disasters.

Spinner: You don't really believe that do you? I saw a fishman fellow from the Neoconland Chicanery Institute think tank on Weasel News the other day and he was saying that those other scientists are fruitcake lefties who got

---

is backward enough to approximate the suppression of accumulating scientific knowledge in the Middle Ages (see McCall, 1979, for details about medieval anti-intellectualism).

their minds warped in the old, corrupt university system. Fortunately, the Great Privatization got rid of all those so-called scientists and replaced them with think-tank graduates.

Splat! A dollop of ideological dung just missed us and hit the wall.

Prober: I'm feeling a little queasy. Can we get out of here?

Spinner: Sure. Let's go through that door into another science lab—the "Invention Laboratory of the Federal Department of Stupor Drugs."

This lab was much cleaner and better equipped than the first. And there were many more scientists, all of whom appeared to be in better spirits than the first ones we visited.

Prober: This place seems a lot friendlier. But why do they call it the Federal Department of Stupor Drugs? We saw Stupor Drug stores and discussed them earlier in the trip. How can a corporation be a government department?

Spinner: It has that name because they sold off all government functions during the Great Privatization[79] a few years ago. They auctioned off the government departments to corporations, wealthy recluses, anyone who could afford to buy a chunk of the government. Great deals, too—three cents on the lucre-buck dollar! So now the old Department of Aggression is owned by Apocalypse Industries, the largest weapons manufacturer in the country.[80] That makes starting and running a war much easier because the Department of Aggression and the weapons manufacturers don't have any communication problems. They *are* the same people in the same executive offices. In fact, as a former business executive himself, the current Emperor knew the motivational value of delegating responsibility so he delegated many of the decisions about going to war to Apocalypse Industries. He kept the decisions about major wars for himself but gave them the power to decide about small to mid-size invasions of the Vassal Lands. It's worked, too, because the number of wars we've fought has escalated considerably in recent years and the efficiency of mobilization has been remarkable. Hats off to the Emperor and the Apocalypse honchos! Later in our trip you'll get to see the

---

79 Privatization has been taken to bizarre extremes. For example, international corporations have been working to privatize the world's drinking water in order to profit handsomely from this vital and hitherto public-domain resource of life (Shiva, 2002). Impoverished people in Bolivia suffered considerably from additional economic hardship while they resisted the expropriation of their own water for resale back to them.

80 Strong ties between elite, corporate interests and the military persist in spite of frequent cautions from prominent Americans throughout history. Two of the most noteworthy red flags came from American presidents: George Washington's denunciations of excessive militarism and Dwight Eisenhower's warnings about the dangers of the military-industrial complex (see Johnson, 2004).

military bases in Wartown. That's one splendid place I tell you. If you don't get excited about things there you won't get excited about anything.

Prober: You said the Department of Aggression. Don't you mean the Department of Defense?

Spinner: No. Department of Defense was the old, old name. They changed it to Department of Aggression to reflect its true purpose. After the population became truly right-thinking through the use of ideological paste from the think tanks, their infatuation with Weasel News, the compliance juice in the schools, and other methods, there was no reason to use the wimpy word "defense" anymore. Now they can call it the Department of Aggression to reflect what it really does, which is to conquer foreign lands for the enrichment of our corporations and the glory of our nation.

Prober: Really? What were some of the other privatization initiatives?

Spinner: Two of the best were the regulatory and education departments. The Anti-Corruption Commission, which makes sure business operations are fair and honest throughout the country, was bought up by Fraudulent Finance, the innovative and aggressive high-interest, hedge fund, loan and credit card people.[81] Obviously, that worked great because there haven't been any corporate corruption scandals since that privatization. Business runs smoothly now, especially the finance industry. In another brilliant acquisition, the old Department of Education was purchased by Loopy Nefarious, a famous televangelist, second only to Abominate Frenzy in popularity. Boy, has he made a difference! Now all the kids get proper values, or else, as you'll see when we visit some schools at our next stop. Anyway, the auction really improved the government because it operates more like a business now.

Prober: OK, how about getting back to science for a minute? Tell me what's going on here in this fancy lab.

Spinner: This is where the really important practical science goes on. That's why the lab is so lavish in comparison with the basic research facility, which tries to discover basic scientific principles—what a waste of time! Also, this newer lab is unregulated so the scientists can really innovate. Notice the absence of monkeymen? Before the Great Deregulation they were even having trouble getting permission to carve up and poison animals, let alone to test on human subjects. Now with deregulation and the new Sentient Being Carve Up laws they can use any experimental procedures they want. See that cage

---

81 Predatory lending is one of the worst forms of exploitation. Lenders target the working poor, the elderly, and other vulnerable groups and lure them into loans with exorbitant interest rates, excessive penalties, and enormous balloon payments that raise the risk of default considerably (see Squires, 2004). In essence, the practice is a reverse Robin Hood initiative because it robs from the poor to further enrich the owners and stockholders of financial institutions.

over there holding that group of miserable misfits? They are human subjects used for testing new drugs. Others are locked up in another facility where they are used for testing new cosmetics.

Prober: How can they possibly use human subjects for experimental chemical and drug research?!

Spinner: Easily. All they do is go to Homeless Alley where we keep all the homeless people, and they offer them a few free meals. There's no shortage of volunteers I tell you. And if they ever do need more, all they do is call up the prison warden and he sends over a paddy wagon full of lifers.

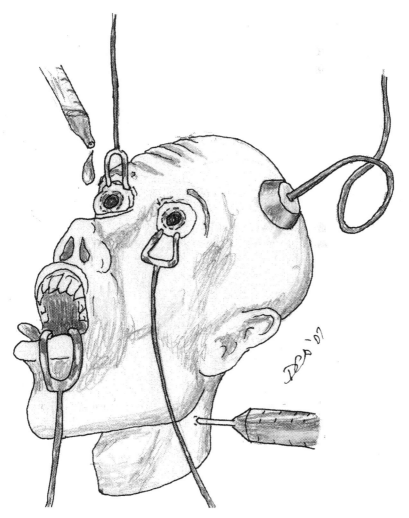

Human Subject Undergoing Drug and Cosmetic Testing in the Laboratories of the Federal Department of Stupor Drugs

Prober: What does important practical science involve?

Spinner: Well, as the sign says, this is where they invent drugs for all sorts of conditions, everything from the common cold to incorrect thinking. Here is where they came up with the compliance juice that's so critical to our education program. You'll soon see the powerful effects of that juice when we visit the schools. Each lab station is dedicated to research on a different ailment or condition. This one here is for obesity. Last year, they invented a pill that blocks the absorption of fat into the body. It also blocks 99% of nutrient absorption, but that's a small price to pay for beauty.

Prober: Maybe you wouldn't need those pills if you didn't get most of your food from those huge factory farms we've seen where the livestock are trapped in pens and cages throughout their short, miserable lives and force fed, drugged, and shot up with hormones to maximize their weight.

Spinner: That's a silly notion. The factory farms are a vital part of our economy and they provide great returns to their owners and investors. They couldn't possibly operate any differently.

Prober: You said each lab station in here is for research on only one or two drugs. I notice that there are some stations around the periphery of the facility, but several stations here in the middle are by far the biggest and have the best equipment. They also have the most scientists working at them. What's so important at these stations that they require the lion's share of resources?

Spinner: Glad you asked. These are the showcase research projects—the ones that will reap the most profit and bring the most benefit to shareholders. The scientists at the second biggest station over there are working on men's hair loss. They're testing all kinds of creams and pills that we hope will keep our men the handsomest in the world. The third biggest station right beside us is where we recently had a couple of huge breakthroughs. You might have noticed that many people in the nation don't have wrinkles on their faces. And many of the women have perfect, enormous breasts, even pre-teen girls and women in their 70s and 80s. These improvements used to come from plastic surgery but not anymore. Now they come from pills! If you take a pill called "Shallowyline" you'll get the perfect skin. And the giant breasts come from a pill called "Elephanesta."[82]

---

82 Vainglorious beauty enhancement has become an enormous industry even though cosmetic surgery is remarkably invasive and expensive. According to Morgan (1994), "Not only is elective cosmetic surgery moving out of the domain of the sleazy, the suspicious, the secretly deviant, or the pathologically narcissistic, *it is becoming the norm* . . . so that women who contemplate *not using* cosmetic surgery will be stigmatized and seen as deviant" (p. 240). In short, the

Prober: You say these are the most important drugs but what about serious diseases? Wouldn't seeking cures for them be more important?

Spinner: It's hard to argue with objective facts. The scientists who invented Shallowyline and Elephanesta both won Slapdash Prizes, which are the most prestigious scientific research awards we have. If those drugs weren't important, their inventors obviously wouldn't be recognized nationally.

Prober: You haven't told me about the biggest lab station in the facility: the one right in the middle with most of the scientists scurrying around it.

Weasel News Reporter Britney Bubblehead Interviewing Socialite Bimbo Jumbobazoom About the Benefits of Elephanesta

various branches of the cosmetic industry have successfully sold women's bodies as profit-generating, aesthetic objects.

Spinner: Ah, that's the most critical research project in the land, attracting the best scientific minds and billions in research grants. Here, they're working on the problem of erectile dysfunction: the scourge of the 21st century. They're making great progress. One drug they invented, called "Spectacular Tumescia," really worked well but when they started marketing it, various appendages began to fall off the customers so they had to recall it and work on it some more. Once they solve that problem the quality of life in the nation will skyrocket! You can bet your bottom lucre-buck dollar they'll win another Slapdash Prize for that!

Prober: Wow! Wouldn't there have been some big lawsuits over that—over the missing appendages, I mean?

Spinner: Not really. You see, the research facility here is a government department but, as I mentioned, it's owned and operated by the big pharmaceutical corporation Stupor Drugs. It's really ingenious you know. The executives at the drug company, along with their friends over at Coughing Coal-Black Industries, paid their lobbyists hundreds of millions; they in turn paid a fraction of that to the politicians they own, who in turn passed the Corporate Protection Act several years ago. Remember, I mentioned this law earlier on the trip? The act makes it illegal to sue any corporation for any reason. A foolish attempt to sue results in a minimum 25 years in prison. Even criticizing a corporation violates a subsection of the act and brings a hefty fine and/or imprisonment. That really put the trial lawyers in their places. Bottom line is, well—the bottom line. This law raised corporate profits and stock prices overnight, making it one of the most brilliant legal innovations of all time.

Prober: But what about the innocent consumer who believes the advertising, takes poisoned pills, and suffers severe health problems as a result?

Spinner: You really didn't learn much from reading the Golden Slab, did you? Those hurt by the effects of a drug weren't taking enough personal responsibility. It's their own fault. On another note, we have to keep you on schedule and our next visit takes us into the school system. If you've been wondering how we've become so efficient here in Neoconland, much of the credit goes to the diligent reformers who gutted the old, ineffective, public school system and built a new, dynamic, private system in its place.

CH 12.

EDUCATING THEIR YOUNG: ASSEMBLY LINE FACTORIES AND LA-DI-DA LEARNING SPAS

On our way to the schools I noticed that there were no school buses on the road and no children skipping along the sidewalks. Spinner told me that all schools now are residential and children are seldom seen anywhere in public during the school year. He also told me that the schools we were visiting today were housed in a single, massive complex so we would be able to see a lot in a short period of time. We had passed by many factories since the beginning of the trip and the enormous factory school off in the distance appeared no different except for the lack of a smokestack spewing toxins into the atmosphere. I wondered what hidden toxins might lurk within.

Spinner: We'll soon be making our way into a state-of-the-art factory school. The kids of the Near Dregs and the Putrid Scum, the ones who don't live on the street and actually attend school, go to that big, old, privatized factory school over there, the one with the huge advertising billboards. You've likely seen it advertised on Weasel network TV. The school has a very long assembly line traveling through three production facilities. First, the kids go through "Submission Elementary School," then "Indoctrination Middle School," and finally a small number of them make it through "Resignation High." Of course, the children of the Splendiferous Bluebloods and the

Insatiable Predators don't come here. They go to a magnificent palace in the foothills of Mt. Exclusion— "Hoity-Toity Château Chic" School.[83]

Prober: Why do you have two very different, segregated school systems?[84]

Spinner: It wasn't always like this. At one time all kids went to public schools that were pretty much the same from one location to another. There wasn't much difference in the experience of a kid in White City compared with one in Toxica if you can believe it. Actually, the change in the school system is one more example of the Emperor's wise leadership. Lobbyists advised him that the old publicly financed schools we used to have in places like FDR Plaza were wasting lots of money on the hopeless brats of Near Dregs and Putrid Scum, and so he should shut them down. In addition, they said if he closed the public schools and made private schools the only option, the stock for private schools would go through the roof and many Splendiferous Blueblood and Insatiable Predator investors would stand to make barrels full of money. Taking their advice, he had his Secretary of Education come up with a way to accomplish the privatization without too much fuss.[85] With the help of the think tanks, they created a new law called "No Child Left

---

83 We tend to assume that education is the great equalizer, creating opportunities for deprived children to rise to higher stations in life. However, Sacks (2007), Oakes (1986), and Kozol (1991, 1995, 2005) showed how the de facto segregation of our school systems reinforces class differences by providing some children with wonderful opportunities in well-funded schools and higher program tracks (options) while locking many others into impoverished, barren, and often dangerous learning environments. Kozol called this inequality a form of apartheid, which has been worsening in recent years. The results for deprived students include protomilitary manipulation and control; punitive evaluation and sorting systems; and intellectually barren instructional methods. The meritocracy in which neoconservatives take such pride is an illusion hiding gross inequalities of opportunity.

84 Hochschild and Scovronick (2003) demonstrated that arguments over the segregation of schooling ultimately come down to arguments favoring either the individual success of privileged children or the collective good of all children. We must not forget the value of a common public education.

85 Privatizers assume that parents and children are "customers" who will benefit from choice, but education is much more than a commodity. Education requires civic engagement (Abernathy, 2005) and privatization of schools drains citizenship from the system leaving only self-interest. Poor children in poor schools suffer the most from this trend. Efforts to privatize schools tend to be ill-conceived and rooted in ignorance while the grandiose claims of educational improvement that accompany them tend not to materialize (see Apple, 2001, 2004; Bracey, 2002; Moffett, 1994; Spring, 2002).

Unscathed" (NCLU) that required all public-school kids, regardless of ability, to be average, and all public schools, regardless of their resources, to make sure that all their kids were average, exactly average according to the rigorous Myopic Standardized Tests,[86] which were designed in the Superficial Surface Skimming think tank. Of course, the educators couldn't meet this goal no matter how hard they tried because the schools had kids with learning disabilities or other problems. For example, most of the kids in Toxica had black-lung disease, lead-paint poisoning, and malnutrition, so many of them couldn't become average no matter what the teachers did.[87] So none of the schools and teachers met the standards and all were labeled failures. Pictures of the failing teachers were advertised publicly alongside posters of wanted criminals and sexual predators. Boy, they really got lambasted! It didn't take long before many of them gave up teaching. The lucky ones found entry-level jobs as greeters in the stores of Big Boxica, or as prison guards in the enormous new prisons the Emperor was building, or they became itinerant gardeners or maids and nannies on the estates of White City. Many others became homeless and soon made their way into the prison system as inmates. Of course, the old schools closed and the Emperor was able to privatize the entire education system. The large factory that now houses Submission Elementary School, Indoctrination Middle School, and Resignation High used to be a cesspool factory, which closed in the outsourcings and downsizings of the last few years. The Rapscallion Corporation, which is owned by the famous televangelist Loopy Nefarious, bought the factory for 3 cents on the lucre-buck dollar, slapped on a coat of gray, industrial paint, and turned it into the wonderful school you see here today. They run it very efficiently: paying the teachers even less than they got before and assigning one teacher for every 600 kids instead of the 1 to 25 inefficiency of the old public system. Those savings mean big profits for the shareholders and there's a lot of money left over for advertising.[88] They started out at a 450 to 1 student-teacher ratio

---

86 Standardized testing has useful diagnostic purposes but it is decidedly NOT suitable as the primary instrument for accountability and reform initiatives (Eisner, 2001; Kohn, 2000; Ohanion, 2001; Thomas & Bainbridge, 2001; Thompson, 2001).

87 The global environmental crisis is damaging the health of all. Children and the working class are the most vulnerable (McCally, 2002).

88 High-profile scholars are very skeptical of claims that market-based school "reforms" will improve education (see Abernathy, 2005; Berliner & Biddle, 1995; Giroux, 1999). Many argue that punitive reforms such as No Child Left Behind are making teaching and learning much more mechanical and superficial while hurting the life chances of deprived children (Apple, 2004, 2005; Bracey, 2002). Much neoconservative school reform is based on deception and biased

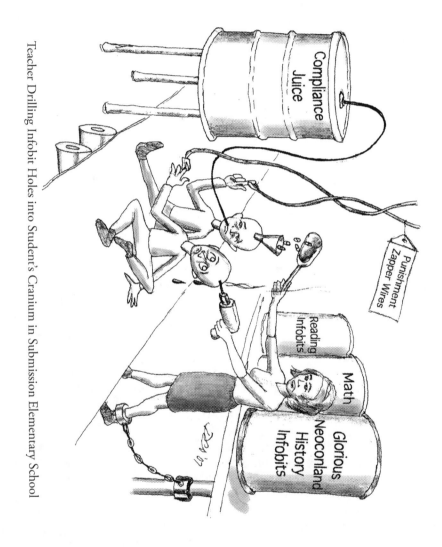

Teacher Drilling Infobit Holes into Student's Cranium in Submission Elementary School

but by moving it up to 600 to 1 they were able to build huge billboards and to run flashy ads on TV every day while increasing shareholder profits even more. Brilliant! Just brilliant! And the standardization is remarkable. Everyone and everything is in lockstep just as NCLU mandated. Let's go in and have a look around.

We pulled up to the factory entrance, which was protected by armed sentries and a locked, iron-barred gate. After going through fingerprinting and searches at a series of checkpoints, we made our way into the bowels of the system that constituted Submission Elementary School. Inside, it took a few minutes to adjust to the dimly lit, smoky, noisy interior. Grease-covered levers, clocks, gears, gauges, and steam-spewing pipes seemed to be everywhere. Thousands of small, frail children sat passively on a large, slow-moving conveyor belt. Every 50 feet or so an adult, an educator-technocrat, stood at the side of the belt operating machinery. Stepping closer to one of these technocrats, I noticed that her leg was chained to the frame of the assembly line and she was using an electric drill to bore a small hole in the skull of a child. Surprisingly, the child seemed to feel nothing. Electrical wires labeled "punishment zappers" extended down from the ceiling and were attached with alligator clips to the child's fingers.[89]

Prober: Ouch! How can they do that drilling? And why isn't the child crying?

Spinner: They have to do it. Otherwise, how would they get the infobit pills into the kids' weak little brains? You don't seem to know much about education, do you? And the drill isn't very painful because the compliance juice is laced with anesthetic.

Prober: What is compliance juice anyway? You've mentioned it several times.

Spinner: The headmaster/CEO found that the kids function better in here if they get a strong dose of compliance juice every day. See that 45-gallon barrel beside the conveyor belt? It's full of juice extracted from the fruit of the servitude tree. It calms the kids, makes them very docile, and inclines them to accept proper values without much complaint. There's plenty of the juice because the Rapscallion Corporation that owns the school also owns most of the servitude tree orchards in the nation. Remember the think tanks we visited? The Dissent Suppression Forum tank mixes a lot of this juice into its ideological paste before it's pumped out into the Weasel News complex, the public drinking fountains, and other places. The juice is great because it

---

89 The punitive atmosphere of the school reflects the reluctance of the neoconservative-dominated American government to accept the United Nations Declaration of the Rights of the Child. As of the early 21st century, the holdouts included the United States and Somalia (Robertson, 2001).

makes the nation more harmonious. Anyway, the headmaster/CEO of the school makes sure the educators force the juice into the kids through the feeding tubes. There's a powerful anesthetic mixed in with the juice to dull any pain that might come from the skull drills or from the pressure ulcers the kids get from sitting still on the conveyor belts for a decade or more.

Prober: You mentioned infobit pills. What are they?

Spinner: They're facts in pill form. Kids need to know facts. For example, they need to know that General Blowhard Swagger was the hero of the last battle in the conquest of the first Vassal Land we invaded. They have to be able to recite what year the intrepid secret-police union-busting unit destroyed the last vestiges of the despicable workers' union in FDR Plaza. They also need a few skills such as mastery of the precise movements needed to prepare and flip a Supersized Megaslopburger most efficiently.[90] The Megaslopburger is the favorite food of the Near Dreg class. Of course, the Splendiferous Blueblood and Insatiable Predator kids at Hoity-Toity Château Chic School learn more advanced skills like the key steps to take in leveraging a hostile takeover of another kid's lemonade stand, or how to hide their inheritances in an off-shore tax haven should that form of taxation ever arise again, God forbid, or how to find an investment broker who can bend the few, limited rules that remain in the financial industry. Each little fact, or each little step of a skill, comes in a capsule. We call these capsules infobits. Each subject area has its own barrel-o-bits. So there's a math barrel, a reading barrel, and a glorious Neoconland history barrel.[91] You can see these barrels behind the teacher here

---

90   While studying the school experiences of working-class boys, Willis (1977) observed that they rejected and subverted the education they were receiving because they saw through the societal system for which school was preparing them, perceiving it as nonmeritocratic and stacked against them. Preparing children for citizenship in a participatory democracy used to be an important goal of education; however, that goal is being replaced by a consumerist vision of children as malleable components of the economic marketplace (Anderson, 1998).

91   There is a disturbing tendency for school "reformers" to oversimplify education. For example, most assume that learning entails the transmission of decontextualized information bits from the teacher into the skull-receptacles of passive students (Bracey, 1987, 2002; Cohen, Higgins, & Ambrose, 1999; Giroux, 1999; Kohn, 2000, 2001; Moffett, 1994; Sizer, 1992; Thomas & Bainbridge, 2001; Zemelman, Daniels, & Hyde, 2005). Such assumptions ignore important cognitive-science research about memory, motivation, and cognitive styles. Neoconservatives attempt to redefine the history curriculum for schools to make it more favorable to their ideology. For example, an array of neoconservative pundits and politicians vehemently denounced a set of new national standards for history in education because they weren't sufficiently aligned with their cause

at the assembly line. A few years ago they threw all the arts barrels in the trash because those bits were totally useless.[92] When teaching, the teacher just scoops up a trowel full of bits from a barrel and pours them into each kid's head via the lecture funnel, which slides neatly into the cranial hole the teachers drilled into each kid's head in the early years of school. Look, the teacher is filling a cranium right now.

Prober: Why are electrical wires attached to the kids' hands?

Spinner: They're a back-up system in case a child happens to be immune to the compliance juice. A few sharp jolts of electricity quickly get kids back in line.[93] But the system is fair. The shackles on the teachers' legs also are

---

(see Symcox, 2002). Much of this inaccuracy and deception has permeated history textbooks for some time. The texts are loaded with distortions while omitting anything that would reflect poorly on the nation's character (Loewen, 1995).

92 The No Child Left Behind (NCLB) legislation, which is primarily a neoconservative brainchild, is chock-full of major flaws, misconceptions, and deceptions that hurt children and undermine true education (see Apple, 2005; Meier & Wood, 2004). Its assumption that punitive accountability based on superficial, standardized measures will improve education is half-baked to say the least. Its requirement that all schools and students meet the same standards in spite of enormous differences in community and school resources, student capabilities, and life circumstances is imprudent at best and looks much like a malicious attempt to "prove" that desperately underfunded public schools are failures in need of privatization. Schools that aren't situated in affluent, suburban neighborhoods are virtually guaranteed to fail. In addition, school-reform initiatives, especially those promoted by neoconservatives, tend to ignore or marginalize the arts in favor of more "important" subjects such as science, mathematics, and literacy. These latter subjects are touted as crucial to "national competitiveness." Nevertheless, the arts enhance learning by developing students' thinking capacities in ways that other subject areas cannot (Eisner, 2002) because artistic work and appreciation exercises the following cognitive capacities, among others: (a) imagination; (b) tolerance of ambiguity; (c) aesthetics and emotion; (d) the capacity for engaging in sophisticated thought experiments conducive to complex problem solving; and (e) the ability to mode switch, which entails translation of concepts from one thought modality or form of representation (visual, verbal, kinesthetic) into another (Ambrose, 1996, 1998; Cohen, 1994; Eisner, 1987, 1993, 2002), Many eminent scientists accomplish their greatest work through visual thinking and mode switching (Miller, 1986, 1989, 1996; West, 1991, 2004).

93 Lakoff (2002) illustrated ways in which metaphors of family dynamics shape our assumptions about social institutions. A strict-father metaphor inclines conservatives to value autocratic, male-dominant institutions whereas a nurturant-family metaphor inclines liberals to value collaborative, democratic

electrified so the CEO can give his employees the occasional reminder about the purpose of education should they go soft and show too much compassion, or should they try to get the kids to think.

Prober: But what about developing purpose, motivation, and creative and critical thinking? Isn't the ability to think and act purposefully in the world an important goal of education?

Spinner: Come on now. Get realistic! Why on earth would you want Near Dreg and Putrid Scum kids to think?! They don't need to think to do the kind of work they're destined to do: you know, cleaning toilets, extracting animal entrails in the slaughterhouses, serving drinks and the like. And if they learned to think they might just become troublemakers, questioning things about our glorious system. They might become immune to the ideological idea fuel from the think tanks. A few might even question the Golden Slab, and we can't have that, can we? It was that kind of education that made the old, public schools so dangerous in the dark days of the early to mid 20th century.

Prober: What happens at the end of the assembly line?

Spinner: That's a great time for the kids, or at least for some of them. Their cranial holes are plugged up because their learning is done. Then they take a multiple-choice test on the facts and skills they learned. The ones who learned best step right onto trains going to places like Big Boxica, White City, or Wretched Warehouse Prison where they start their jobs as clerks in the stores, servants or gardeners on the estates, or guards in the prisons. Those who don't pass the exams are herded onto buses that take them either to Wartown for basic military training or out into Homeless Alley, which ultimately funnels them into the prison where they'll enter as inmates.

Prober: *[astonished]* You've mentioned Homeless Alley several times.[94] Why do you have a special, run-down alley designated for homeless people, and why do they go to prison if they haven't committed a crime?

Spinner: Everyone knows that these kids, especially the Putrid Scum kids, will end up in prison anyway if they don't pass these exams. It's just more efficient and humane if they don't go into the regular streets of the nation where they would bother respectable citizens. Herding them all into a

---

decision making. Cross and Cross (2005) showed how these metaphors compete for dominance in the education system with strict-father dynamics prevailing where schools emphasize strict accountability, punishment, and individual competition. Punishment zappers and compliance juice would be somewhat extreme but logical extensions of neoconservative school-reform arguments.

94 Homelessness is a serious, under-addressed social problem, and the homeless face a daunting array of related problems such as malnutrition, untreated health conditions, and early mortality (see Sidel & Levy, 2006).

special, designated, walled-off homeless alley where nobody has to see them just makes the streets so much nicer. And since they'll eventually end up in jail anyway, the Emperor made homelessness a felony; that way, they go to jail rather quickly and automatically after a few weeks instead of hanging around out there suffering too long and eventually committing more serious crimes. See how brilliant that is? Hey, it's time to get out of here and see a real school, one where our kids really learn. We're off to Hoity-Toity Château Chic prep academy.

Glad to escape the oppressive dinginess of Submission Elementary School, we got back into the SUV, left the crowded grimy flatlands, and headed up into the foothills of Mt. Exclusion. Within a few minutes, a carved, marble sign carrying the school name announced our destination. Passing between the pillars of a large stone and wrought-iron gate we cruised along a broad driveway lined with marble statues of former Emperors, famous lobbyists, and think-tank fishmen. The school was a magnificent example of Baroque architecture with opulent, marble ornamentation everywhere. Inside, enormous windows, vaulted ceilings, and impressive frescoes provided an awe-inspiring first impression. As we passed through the 200-foot long foyer on our way to visit with the Headmaster, we saw a few children practicing violin concertos in orchestra pits. Others were sitting in leather-upholstered easy chairs clicking away on big-screen laptop computers. Each child enjoyed the guidance of several teachers who were hovering about making suggestions, bringing resources from the library, and even ghost writing assignments. At the end of the foyer, we were greeted by the Headmaster, a craggy old gentleman decked out in a flowing, black academic gown, barrister's wig, and mortarboard. Under his regalia, I could make out the telltale signs of a past think-tank career: the rudimentary gills, scales, and fin-like arms protruding from the sleeves.

Spinner: Mr. Prober, please say hello to Dr. Starchy Supercilious, Headmaster of Hoity-Toity Château Chic School. Dr. Supercilious is well known throughout the land, not only for his leadership of our finest educational institution but also for his past work at the Superficial Surface Skimming think tank. He wrote some very influential books including *Forget About Learning: Measure and Indoctrinate*, which jump-started the standardized-testing, educational accountability movement. Another of his books, titled *Chain 'Em Up: They're Useless Anyway*, helped justify the movement to de-professionalize public-school teaching and to turn teachers into robot-like technocrats.[95] That saved many millions of lucre-buck dollars and rendered educators compliant so they couldn't make any more silly, baseless complaints about our educational reforms being banal, superficial, and corrupt. Yet another of his books helped us get rid of the professors from the old, liberal universities. That one was titled *The 35 Worst, Evil, Demonic, Wacko Professors.*[96]

Prober: Pleased to make your acquaintance Dr. Supercilious.

Starchy: I'm sure. How do you like our school?

Prober: Wow! These kids really get the attention, don't they!

Starchy: Oh yes. We make sure that each child has several personal teachers and tutors who serve as research assistants and general gofers.

Prober: How do you recruit your faculty and students?

Starchy: We don't have to recruit. All citizens want their children enrolled here. We're very selective about admissions. First, candidates have to pass a subset of the Myopic Standardized Tests, which are sold by my former institution, the Superficial Surface Skimming think tank. For the children, we use two tests. We do our first screening with the Legacy Back Door Assessment, which tests for appropriate family background and whether or not the child's surname is related to our endowment in any significant way.[97] Those who pass this test are admitted and assigned the best teachers and

---

95 A number of would-be school reformers downplay the importance of professional teaching methods acquired in teacher preparation programs (e.g., Finn, 2008; Ravitch, 2000). If they have their way, teaching will become even more mechanical, robotic, and technocratic.

96 Horowitz (2006), a conservative ideologue, published a book severely criticizing the 101 worst professors in our universities in an attempt to inject more right-wing extremist thought into university campuses. He aimed his venom at cherry-picked scholars from the social sciences and humanities. Revealing the superficiality of his analysis, his argument missed the nature of much social-science research, which is to investigate the social, cultural, political, and economic contexts of society. Such investigation is bound to turn up power imbalances and injustices. These findings look like liberal bias to narrow-minded, short-sighted, right-wing extremists. In short, social scientists typically aren't flaming liberals who make up unjust criticism of a virtuous, utopian, conservative society. Instead, their findings tend to reveal serious flaws in the simplistic, utopian assumptions, arguments, and actions of right-wing extremists.

97 Elite schools and universities began the practice of legacy admissions to give the children of wealthy, white families an advantage in the admission process, because children of immigrants were outperforming them on admission tests. While the practice has abated somewhat it remains alive and well. Overall, it represents a deliberate lowering of standards to maintain class- and race-based discrimination (Kivel, 2002).

tutors. They automatically go into our gifted and talented program track. Those who don't pass get a second chance by taking the TriviaFacto Battery, which tests for knowledge of the Golden Slab and other important facts about our glorious history. We always find a few children with hidden potential by skimming off those who score above average on the TriviaFacto tests. For the teachers, they have to pass the Loyal Lackey Tests, which ensure that our educators are malleable employees with impeccable character.

Teacher Serving a Student at Hoity-Toity Château Chic School

Prober: All the students I've seen since we arrived have been boys. Don't you have girls in the school?

Starchy: We have some on the kitchen staff but not in the student body. Heavens no! There are other schools for them.

Prober: Where do your students go when they graduate?

Starchy: Virtually all of them go on to Dogma University. As you can see from the statues lining our driveway, our graduates include a long list of great achievers in government, industry, and the military.

Prober: Please forgive me. I have to be honest. On the way in I noticed that many of your students didn't look all that intelligent. One of them was drooling on his exam paper while his tutor filled in the multiple-choice bubbles for him. Another misspelled a four-letter profanity as he was carving it into that oak table over there. Several others were off in the corner having a flatulence contest.

Starchy: *[testily]* I can tell you aren't very familiar with the subtleties of education. The proof is in the pudding. For years now, every single student who has passed the Legacy Back Door test has graduated with flying colors. And all of our graduates have gained degrees at Dogma University. I don't think you have any basis for your specious criticism.

Prober: OK, pardon my impertinence. Another question. Other than the sculptures and frescos in your magnificent building, I didn't see any evidence of students engaged in the arts. What are your arts programs like?

Starchy: The arts aren't important so they aren't in our curriculum. Of course, there are exceptions such as those students playing their violins in the foyer. But we just have them do that for show, for the ambience. *[checking his pager]* Oh, my assistant just notified me that one of our most important benefactors is on his way. Ha ha! Here goes our endowment again, through this lofty, vaulted ceiling! I must go now. If you haven't already been there, why don't you drop by Resignation High School so you can compare? I'm sure you'll be singing our praises after that.

Our next stop was Wretched Warehouse Prison, by far the largest correctional facility in the world.

CH 13.

WRETCHED WAREHOUSE PRISON

As we approached the prison its sheer size staggered me, dwarfing anything I had seen on this trip or any other. It's stark gray stone walls stretched out past the horizon and each of the many imposing watchtowers was over 100' tall. Chillingly, Dante's inscription at the entrance to hell—"Abandon all hope ye who enter here"—was emblazoned in bright-red paint on a wooden sign hung over the main gate. After passing through a series of checkpoints and inspections, we met with the warden, Malign Lout, a surly, rotund fellow with cauliflower ears and a considerable crust of scar tissue around his eyes.

Spinner: Hello Warden Lout. Thanks for taking time from your busy day to visit with us.

Malign: *[growling]* You're not a couple of bleeding heart liberals, are you? Last time I met with foreigners they seemed to want me to throw open the gates and let all these scurvy scum out on the streets.

Spinner: On no. We've heard so much about your prison and we just want to see how you operate it.

Malign: All right then, let's make our way up into the central watchtower.

We took an elevator to the top of the tower and stepped out onto a circular platform bristling with machine guns, searchlights, and telescopes. Scores of beefy guards were diligently watching the few steel doors and barred windows in each of the many cellblocks of the complex.

Malign Lout: Warden at Wretched Warehouse Prison

Prober: This is a very large facility. How many inmates do you have here?

Malign: At last count we had about 14 million prisoners plus or minus a few million. If we were a city we would be the largest urban region in the country by far. Pretty good, huh?[98]

Prober: That's astounding! Why are there so many prisoners?

Malign: The main reason is the Putrid Scum and the Near Dregs who befoul our great nation with their very existence. Most of their kids find their way here in very short order once the schools are done babysitting them.[99]

---

98 America has an enormous, overcrowded prison system and the highest incarceration rate in the developed world, yet the system still has been ineffective in suppressing crime (Skolnick, 1997). Laws aimed at getting tough on crime have little effect on rates of violent crime (Zimring & Hawkins, 1999).

99 Lower-class people who have committed petty crimes fill the prisons while white-collar criminals face incarceration only on very rare occasions. This represents a

We also have a lot of new laws that bring in more inmates. There's the Anti-Loitering law, which sends homeless scum to prison if they linger in Homeless Alley for more than a few weeks. But why wait a few weeks? It should kick in after a few hours if you ask me—the vile lowlifes. The Environmental Loonie Law used to bring us a lot of crazy tree huggers who ran around in the woods doing who knows what. But they've reduced to a trickle because there aren't many forests anymore. The Sentient Being Carve Up laws give our pharmaceutical and cosmetic companies the right to do any research they like on animals and Putrid Scum human subjects so any runaway human research subjects end up here, along with anyone who helps them. And then there's the more general Corporate Protection Act that carries lengthy sentences for criticizing our infallible corporations.

Prober: Please excuse me but you were just badmouthing the Near Dregs and I see you have a skull and crossbones, the Near Dreg birth symbol, tattooed on your wrist.

Malign: *[angrily]* I thought you said you weren't a bleeding heart liberal! Here, look closer. My wrist has an RWA tattooed over the skull and crossbones, canceling it out!

Prober: Pardon me, I didn't mean to offend. What does RWA mean?

Malign: Right-Wing Authoritarian, of course. I'm an RWA. It's an honorable sign indicating that I passed the indoctrination courses for supervisory work as a guard in the prison system, or a noncommissioned officer in the military, or a military policeman, or a foreman in a factory. Not only that, I'm also a Double High, which is the strongest form of RWA because Double Highs make great leaders. I'm the highest-ranking former Near Dreg in the country. You might say I'm proof the Neoconian dream is alive and well.

Prober: Tell me more about what it takes to be an RWA.

Malign: Becoming an RWA is a wonderful thing and it's about the only way a Near Dreg can make it in today's world. You have to be nominated by an important person in your community and then you go away to an ideological boot camp out in the wilderness. They test you a lot with survival games and role-playing, things like that. They're looking for several key characteristics. First, they want you to follow orders without question. If you're the kind of person who will jump off a cliff because your leader says so, you'll make good points on their scorecards. Second, they want you to defend your leaders with aggressive violence no matter what they do, especially when they're accused of heinous crimes by lying, low-life progressives. You have to be all in, no

---

serious injustice because white-collar crime causes far more damage to society than does petty street crime (Meltzer, 1990).

ifs, ands, or buts. And your aggression has to come from the gut. You have to be absolutely certain about the correctness of your own position. Third, you have to be decisive, immediately, no wishy-washy flip-flopping! You have to see every issue instantly in black and white. There is no gray. Fourth, you must not tolerate foreign ideas or people, even a smidgen. Feminists, multiculturalists, intellectuals, and homosexuals must generate such fear and loathing in your gut that you'll do anything to destroy them, and I mean anything![100] My RWA friends and I proudly wear our tattoos. Some of us meet in our White Bulls of Revulsion clubhouse on weekends, put on our white-sheet costumes and our big, plastic bull gonads and then burn things while we chant our RWA slogans. Membership is quite an honor, I tell you. Well, let's move on. It's time to tour the cellblocks.

---

100 Various scholars have studied the thoughts and motivations behind the forms of social dominance that enable vile leaders such as Adolf Hitler and other fascists to gain and abuse power (e.g., Sidanius and Pratto, 2001). Racism, patriarchy, and classism are sustained and invigorated by such leaders. Through extensive psychological research, Altemeyer (1996, 1999, 2004; Altemeyer & Hunsberger, 2005) discovered patterns of right-wing-authoritarian (RWA) thought and motivation. RWAs (a) are loyally submissive to authorities who hold beliefs similar to their own, (b) unquestioningly follow their leaders' suggestions or commands, (c) are dogmatic and will aggressively attack those who criticize their leaders, (d) easily shed guilt when they use aggressive violence because their dogmatism arises from fear and a sense of deep-seated, self-righteous moral superiority, (e) show extreme intolerance and a willingness to severely punish those whose beliefs or behaviors differ from their own (e.g., people from foreign cultures, feminists, homosexuals), and (f) are prone to hypocrisy because their sheep-like tendency to follow authority figures robs them of critical thinking capacities while making them unaware of their own prejudices. Double highs are variants of the RWAs but they are much more inclined to enjoy dominating others. They will engage in aggressive, domineering, and malicious behaviors to manipulate or coerce others with little moral restraint, often going to great lengths in attempts to get away with immoral or illegal actions. Moreover, they adhere to conservative political, economic, and religious fundamentalist perspectives but use religion as a tool for manipulation, not as a personal moral compass. Traditional conservatives are much more reasonable and moderate so they often find the actions of double highs abhorrent. The combination of numerous sheep-like, intolerant, violence-prone RWAs and a few influential, unscrupulous, manipulative double-high leaders represents a dangerous, inflammatory situation for a society. Some neoconservative policies and actions seem well aligned with the thoughts and behaviors of double highs (e.g., preemptive war, abusing prisoners).

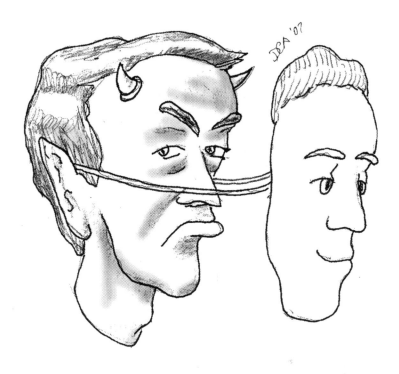

Unmasked Right-Wing Authoritarian: Possibly a Double High

Malign's description of RWAs reminded me of the frightening photograph another reporter e-mailed me just before she disappeared never to be heard from again (Sorry, I can't bring myself to tell you what was in the photo.) The reporter, Patricia Plucky, was an ascending journalist at the Neutral Lands Gazette *and she courageously made an earlier investigative trip to Neoconland. Being a woman, she had a very difficult time getting a visa and gaining access to important locations like I did on this later trip. But she was assertive and persuasive enough to make it into a few interesting spots. The last time we heard from her she had broken into a secret clubhouse of some kind and hid in a closet hoping to get the scoop on a meeting of bulls. I'm pretty sure she mentioned the White Bulls of Revulsion. I still recall the message that accompanied the photo. It went something like this: "You won't believe these guys! They put on civilized faces in public but when they relax the masks come off, and it's not a pretty picture." That was the last we heard from her.[101] Lacking Patricia Plucky's courage, I decided not to ask any questions about the club, not while I was visiting a prison run by Warden Lout.*

We took the elevator to the ground floor and then made our way across the concrete yard into a cellblock, which was locked down tighter than Fort Knox. The mold-covered, vermin-infested hallway was lit with a few bare, flickering 40-watt bulbs hanging from the ceiling. We stopped at a rusty cell door and Malign pulled open a small shutter. Peering inside I could just make out a pathetic, scrawny, near-naked, shivering figure chained to the wall, hanging from his shackled wrists with his toes just touching the floor. There were oozing welts from a whipping over much of his body. The cell wasn't much bigger than a closet.[102]

Prober: He must have done something awful to deserve that punishment. Did he start a fight in the yard? Did he attack a guard or murder another inmate? When will you take him down from his chains?

Malign: That's standard practice. We do that with all our prisoners because it keeps them out of trouble. But don't get your shorts in a knot. We let them down for one hour a day because the prison chaplain insists on it. I hate to say it but I think we need another chaplain. This one just doesn't have enough fire and brimstone.

Prober: What's with the whippings?

Malign: That's a weekly treatment just to let them know who's boss.

Prober: Seems a bit harsh don't you think?

Malign: There you go again. Why don't you mushy liberals just stay away from here if you're so afraid of what goes on?

Prober: If you don't mind, I have another question. The prisoners don't seem to have anything to do because they're locked in the hole 23 hours a day. What about rehabilitation?

---

101 Investigative journalists tend to disappear in Russia (Collings, 2001), which, after the collapse of the Soviet Union, shifted dramatically from extreme, communist, left-wing ideology toward extreme right-wing gangster capitalism (Meier, 2003; Satter, 2003). Gangster capitalists don't like any illumination of their shady dealings. In Mexico, another Darwinian right-wing nation, the human rights lawyer Digna Ochoa was kidnapped and abused several times before being assassinated for working to correct injustices against powerless and deprived populations (Diebel, 2005).

102 Corresponding with the rise of neoconservative influence in the past several decades, the United States Supreme Court has eroded legal protections against cruel and unusual punishment during detention. Dayan (2007) argued that this erosion greased the skids for our moral descent into the acceptance and use of torture as revealed by the abominable practices at Abu Ghraib and Guantánamo. Dehumanization and inhumane punishment are entrenched in our enormous penal system.

Malign: The prisoners you see in this cellblock are new. They'll spend the first few years locked in their holes to get used to the prison. Also, we don't want them talking with each other because that just leads to trouble. Later, they'll go to work on the corporate chain gangs. They'll have plenty to do then working 18 hours a day 7 days a week picking vegetables in the factory farm fields, clearing brush in the ditches, and shoveling coal in the mines for Coughing Coal-Black Industries. All of this is very good for the economy because it lowers prices and maximizes shareholder profit. All that free, forced labor keeps corporate profits high and prices down. For example, in the old days, Coughing Coal-Black Industries had to pay workers minimum wage to shovel coal. Now that they get the chain-gang labor, all they pay are transportation costs to and from the mines. They're even finding more innovative ways to trim costs. They're setting up cots in the mineshafts so they never have to bring the prisoners up to the surface. That saves them transportation costs while cutting down on the number of cellblocks we have to build.

As for rehabilitation, think about it. Most of these criminals come from Putrid Scum stock so they have an inborn lack of intelligence and morals. I wager that none of them can recite more than 3 or 4 of the rules on the Golden Slab even though they spent years in the schools having their heads filled with the correct infobits. In view of all this, what good would rehabilitation do? Spending money on that would be like flushing it down the toilet. Let's move on. Now we're in the capital-punishment wing. There usually are a few good executions going on just about any time of the day so let's step inside the Extermination Amphitheater.

Making our way inside I saw several prisoners being readied for execution. One was tied to a stake with firewood piled around him in preparation for burning. Another was positioned under the gleaming blade of a guillotine, which was dripping crimson from its last job. A third was standing against a bullet-riddled, blood-soaked wall facing a firing squad. But most unusual of all, each of these events was situated in a ring as part of a three-ring circus-like show with a large, cheering crowd and several television film crews from Weasel News.[103]

Prober: I knew you did executions here but I had no idea they were public spectacles.

---

103 Public displays of severe punishment were used as tools of social control in the Middle Ages. For example, along with paranoiac spy systems in which citizens and family members informed on one another, public burning at the stake was a common, horrific, public spectacle used to bring populations into compliance with the dictates of church authorities (Pérez, 2006). We have not regressed that far but public executions would not be incompatible with the beliefs and behaviors of right-wing authoritarians.

Malign: Oh yeah, executions are big entertainment throughout the country, near the top of the ratings for the Weasel TV network. They always bring in big paying crowds here in the amphitheater and that really helps with our operating costs. They're also excellent deterrents because future criminals just have to turn on Weasel News to see what's in store for them down the road. Also, along with our corporate chain gangs, they reduce the prison population, and we need these reductions because we get thousands of new prisoners every day. Even though we're always building new cellblocks we have trouble keeping up, especially since they built Homeless Alley and attached it right to our prison so the homeless could be herded in here and kept off the street.

Prober: I thought nobody used these forms of execution anymore. Some of them seem quite medieval.

Malign: Hey, they work very well and they're very entertaining. If you could stay and watch you would see. But maybe you should come back next Thursday when we have our weekly gladiator night. Execution fans have to put their names in at least a year in advance to get theater seats for those because they're in such hot demand. We borrowed the idea from the ancient Romans so you'll see hundreds of condemned prisoners torn apart by lions. We have 15 of the last 25 remaining lions in the world since they came near extinction. But the real fun is watching the prisoners fight the hopeless psychopaths in the ultimate survival contest. If a prisoner survives, his death sentence is commuted to life imprisonment. When our first Emperor closed down the government insane asylums during the Great Privatization, we had to figure out what to do with the criminally insane psychopaths they let loose on the streets. Our second Emperor came up with a great solution—round them up, bring them here to our gladiator training camps, and then have them fight the condemned in the arena—another win-win solution for our nation. We contain and reduce two troublesome populations while making huge entertainment profits for the Weasel Network. Gladiator night is so successful that it now has surpassed NBL baseball and Wildbelly Wrestling as the most popular sport in the nation.

Oh, time is running short. So come along. We have one more stop: the Organ Harvesting Lab. . . . Here we are now.

Inside the lab, scores of wretches were lying on gurneys and operating tables. Some were cadavers and others were alive. The latter were tied down with leather straps. Doctors were cutting incisions and lifting out kidneys, livers, hearts, and other organs.

Prober: Why is this medical facility part of your prison complex?

Malign: This is another example of the market efficiency that makes our nation the greatest place on earth to live. Those prisoners you saw in the

Extermination Amphitheater will be moved in here when the show's over so we can harvest their organs. The live patients you see here on the operating tables also are prisoners. Some of them volunteer to give up their organs because it reduces their sentences.[104] A kidney is worth 3 years. You get 8 years off for a lung. Some others are losing organs as punishment for breaking prison rules. This is a very efficient operation—pardon the pun. This operating room connects the prison with the finest hospital in the land so the organs are available any time. That enables the doctors to do emergency transplant jobs. For example, only last week one of the leading executives from Coughing Coal-Black industries came in needing a lung transplant so we picked out a prisoner, wheeled him in here, and had the job done in under an hour. Bet you won't see that any place else in the world.

Well, this has been fun but I have to get back to the office and sign a few hundred death warrants for the coming week. If you like, I can get you into the hospital next door. The fellow who owns the hospital owes me big time because I give him great deals on the organ harvesting.

Spinner: That would be great! We have an hour before we have to head off to Wartown. Warden Lout, thank you very much for such an interesting tour of your impressive prison. I sure can see why you became the top-ranked former Near Dreg in the land because you do amazing work here.

---

104 There is much market pressure encouraging the harvesting of organs from powerless, deprived populations for the benefit of affluent individuals in need of transplants. This trend carries serious ethical implications (Price, 2000).

CH 14.

TAKING OUR MEDICINE
IN LUCRATIVE HOSPITAL

Warden Lout made a quick call and an intern physician led us through a short corridor from the prison to the parking-lot basement of the hospital. We waited at an elevator with a building directory posted beside the door. The directory listed the following floors:

1. *Insurance Offices and Emergency Admissions Screening*
2. *Out-Out Patient Handling Ward*
3. *Operating Rooms*
4. *Intensive Care Ward*
5. *Recovery Spa Ward*

As we stepped out of the elevator at the first floor, a big advertising poster greeted us in the lobby. It featured a very handsome pearly-toothed doctor saying, "Welcome to Lucrative Hospital, the best facility in the best medical system in the world! Our motto is—We Care!" A vandal had added the words "about your wallet" in permanent marker at the end of the motto. The Emergency Ward occupied most of the first floor but it differed considerably from anything I had seen back home. Instead of orderlies, interns, and triage nurses, this ward was dominated by accountants wearing three-piece suits and sitting behind desks while they interviewed patients. We stood and watched for a moment. At a desk labeled

"Intake Station 17," a well-dressed man complained about a tummy ache and the emergency-room accountant at the desk asked to see his wrist tattoo and his wallet. Satisfied that the patient was an Insatiable Predator with an overflowing wallet, the accountant gave him a green wristband imprinted with lucre-buck dollar signs and signaled for two orderlies to bring over a gurney. They quickly checked the patient's vital signs and whisked him away to the Intensive Care Ward. Immediately, another patient approached the station. This young fellow was grimacing in pain and holding his wrist, which was protruding from a blood-soaked shirtsleeve at an odd angle. I felt faint when I noticed that the bones of his forearm were protruding through the flesh. The accountant complained that he couldn't see the man's wrist tattoo because of the blood so he asked to see the other wrist. After gently and painfully resting his broken arm on his lap, the young man used his teeth to pull up the sleeve on his good arm revealing the Near Dreg tattoo on his left wrist. The accountant pointed at a sign down a hallway and gave the patient directions to the Common Treatment Courtyard.

Prober: Can we follow the patient? I would like to see what "common treatment" entails.

Spinner: Yes, but we have to check in here first as visitors.

It took a few minutes to check in and pay our rather exorbitant visitors' fees so the patient was gone by the time we were ready to follow. But the trail of his blood led us through a labyrinth of hallways out into a large, concrete yard full of injured and ill patients. Many were lying on the pavement. Some were leaning up against the walls. An orderly with a bullhorn walked through the crowd exhorting them to stand up. When all of the patients had managed to struggle painfully to their feet, even those with broken legs, a couple of workers dressed in Hazmat protective suits walked through the courtyard spraying green and yellow mist all over the crowd. Many of the patients started coughing and some fell back to the ground.

Prober: What are they doing?!

Spinner: Haven't you ever been an outpatient at a hospital before? They're treating them for whatever ails them. The green mist is a powerful disinfectant and the yellow is an all-purpose antibiotic. Those two treatments cover just about any condition a patient might have and mass spraying the patients in a crowd like this is a relatively cost-effective method of treatment that maximizes profit for the shareholders and keeps the hospital stock high. The antibiotic is particularly cost effective because they get it from the cattle industry.

Prober: But what about the man with the broken arm? I see other patients out here with broken bones. Don't they need treatment beyond an aerial spraying?

Prober: Yes, but when the mist settles you'll see some candy striper volunteers wandering through the crowd, selecting those with broken bones, setting the breaks, and applying splints. Those who can afford air splints pay for them and have them installed on the spot. Those who can't afford the air splints get the alternative splints made of duct tape and rolled-up magazines. They're actually pretty effective, or at least that's what they say on Weasel News. We should move on so you can see other parts of the facility.

Applying Disinfectant and Antibiotics in the Common Treatment Courtyard of Lucrative Hospital

Heading back into the building, we passed a long table where volunteers were painstakingly pulling apart medicinal capsules, removing the granules, dividing

them into little piles, and putting a couple on each of many pieces of sticky tape. Near-Dreg and Putrid-Scum patients were standing in a long waiting line. Each time an impatient volunteer called out "Next!" on her bullhorn, a patient would limp forward and take his or her turn at licking the granules off one of the sticky tape pieces.

Spinner: Here's another reason the hospital is so profitable. By dividing up the medication from the capsules and then running the patients through this quick-moving treatment line they get several thousand treated in a day. Even though these patients can pay only a couple of lucre-buck dollars each, it really adds up.[105]

Prober: OK, we've seen many people undergoing treatment, sort of. But we haven't seen a real doctor. Where are they, on the golf course?

Spinner: Ha, ha! Good one. You haven't seen them because they're all upstairs in Intensive Care and the Spa Ward taking care of the important patients.

Prober: Don't the patients down here also need doctors?

Spinner: Hey, you deserve what you pay for. Besides, if they put doctors down here they would have to hire more and they're expensive! That would be a huge strain on Lucrative Hospital's bottom line. Let's go up to the third floor where they do the surgery.

As we stepped out of the elevator we heard some frightful shrieking emanating from behind one of the operating-room doors.

Prober: What's going on in there?!

Spinner: They must be operating on a Near Dreg. Most of them can't afford operations but they sometimes qualify for one if they sell all of their assets and scrape up their life savings and the savings of their friends and relatives. However, they usually can't afford the whole package so they have to cut corners. The patient in there likely couldn't afford the services of an anesthesiologist so he's going without painkiller. In those cases the operating team just straps the patient down and put on their earplugs.

Prober: Wow! That sounds cruel!

Spinner: It isn't cruel at all. It's the patient's choice. If he wants to pay for the anesthetic they'll give it to him.

Prober: I noticed that all patients are wearing green fanny packs with lucre-buck dollar signs on them. What's with that?

---

105 As mentioned in chapter three, our privatized health-care system provides excellent care for some patients but does little to nothing for many others. Lasser, Himmelstein, and Woolhandler (2006) found that the American medical system stacks up poorly against those in other developed nations despite being the most expensive in the world. In spite of this evidence, neocons loudly and religiously sing the praises of privatized medicine.

Spinner: The Admissions accountants make sure they wear them because the hospital takes cash only. They got burned with some fake credit cards a while back. When they're admitted, the patients put all their cash in the fanny pack so they can purchase hospital services whenever they need them. It's really quite efficient. For example, if a patient who has been able to afford anesthesia is unconscious on the operating table and the surgeon comes across a complication that wasn't pre-approved by the accountants for treatment, they wake him up so he can pull out another wad of lucre-buck dollars. There's always an accountant on duty in every operating room in case of fiscal emergencies like this. Then they put him under again and go back to work. Following this protocol causes intense pain while they're making the transaction but without the fanny-pack money, the surgeons would have to complete the first procedure, sew up the patient, wait for him to recover, and then go back in to take care of the complication they discovered. Obviously, that would be far less efficient and much more traumatic for the patient. Oh, look at the time! Come on Mr. Prober, let's head back to the SUV so we can get to Wartown on time. Those military folk don't like tardiness.

Outside we saw hundreds of groggy patients being wheeled out into a parking lot behind the hospital. The orderlies were helping them off the gurneys and seating them on benches or on the ground. Some of the patients were bleeding from their fresh incisions. One of the scurrying orderlies stopped long enough to explain that these were post-op patients who were being turfed out immediately after their operations because they didn't have enough money in their fanny packs to afford time in the recovery wards.

It shocked me to see surgery patients awakening from their invasive procedures and trying to "recover" on the dirty parking-lot pavement. But the scene beyond the hospital property was even more distressing. A chain-link fence topped with razor wire separated the hospital from a crowd of many thousands of seriously injured and ill Neoconians who were begging with tin cups and thronging around any vehicles that entered the facility.[106] Spinner explained that these were the uninsured who didn't have two lucre-buck dollars to rub together. The hospital had to install the razor-wire fence to keep out the beggars because they had been upsetting the paying customers. But there was no time for us to dawdle. Spinner pushed me into the SUV and we sped off to the northwest.

---

106 According to the Institute of Medicine Committee on Assuring the Health of the Public in the 21st Century (2003), the government is responsible for providing health care and protecting the people's health, which is a public good. Unfortunately, well over 40 million Americans are uninsured, and 1 in 4 of the uninsured are children. In addition, many others are vulnerable. Over 70 million lack health insurance for sustained periods of time.

── CH 15. ──

BEATING THE DRUMS IN WARTOWN

I could tell we were approaching Wartown when we passed through villages with names like Slaughterville, Conquer, Subjugatia, and Vanquishville. As we progressed, large military vehicles began to dominate the roadway forcing us to weave through convoys of half-track troop carriers, tanks, armored ammunition supply vehicles, jeeps, self-propelled missile launchers, tanker trucks, camouflaged Earth Devastators, and other vehicles that I couldn't identify. The roadsides were covered with billboards, all featuring rugged-looking soldiers with captions like "Join the many proud warriors. Slaughter 'em all! Whack and conquer! Butcher with the best!"[107] The base itself was a complex of large office buildings and warehouses surrounded by thousands of pup tents covering the ground as far as the eye could see.

Prober: Why are there so many tents here?

Spinner: Impressive, huh? Those are tent cities where all the enlisted soldiers live. They used to house them in barracks but that made them too

---

107 Americans have fallen prey to militarism blended with blind faith in neoconservative utopian ideology (Bacevich, 2005). This dangerous combination inclines us to support costly, bloody, perpetual wars with the intent of imposing a warped version of American values on foreign peoples. A new brand of American imperialism increasingly portrays the use of military power as an acceptable and even preferred foreign policy option for the exercise of power throughout the world (Bacevich, 2002).

soft, and it was too expensive. Turning the barracks into weapon-storage facilities and moving the soldiers into the tents killed two birds with one stone. It made the soldiers a lot tougher because they live in the tents in all kinds of weather throughout their 20-year terms, and it enabled the brass to divert the money they used to spend housing the troops into the production of new weapons. That works great for Apocalypse Industries, the corporation that owns the military, because they make tons of money selling weapons to themselves and paying for them with taxpayers' money.[108]

Prober: It must be hard living in a tent for 20 years.

Spinner: Yes, that's what makes our soldiers the toughest in the world—that along with our innovative training practices. Much of the training involves real fighting with live ammo so some of the recruits die on the practice fields every day. Talk about authentic training! To make it even more real, they lob mortars into the tent cities at night to keep the recruits on their toes.

Prober: Isn't that kind of harsh?

Spinner: Yes, but the survivors are excellent soldiers. They know they're living on borrowed time because they could die any day in training, so it makes them less afraid to take chances in battle. Running through a hail of bullets is second nature to them. And, except for the officers, all the recruits come from the lower classes, the Near Dregs and the Putrid Scum, so they would grow up in harsh conditions even if they weren't in the military; their lives are cheap in places like Toxica.[109] Actually, their life expectancy improves when they join the military because many of them die young in their home cities. They get three squares a day and medical care here.[110]

---

108 American governments have a history of invading nations and/or overthrowing their regimes to serve the political and economic ends of powerful interest groups (Kinzer, 2003, 2006). These regime changes often advance the interests of corporations. Examples include the overthrow of a democratic regime in Guatemala for the benefit of a produce corporation and a democracy in Iran for the benefit of western oil companies. The subsequent imposition of dictatorships in these and other nations consolidated our corporate gains.

109 In nations with extreme socioeconomic inequality such as the United States, people have shorter life spans in comparison with those living in more egalitarian nations such as Japan or Sweden (Wilkinson, 2001). Wilkinson argued that gross inequality is new to our species, manifesting in the human race for only a few thousand years—a very short time in the history of human existence. Since we've had insufficient time for evolutionary adaptation to these foreign conditions, those at the bottom of extreme hierarchies suffer from the debilitating stress of harsh environments ill-suited to human well-being.

110 Farmer (2003), a medical anthropologist, analyzed the health problems of poverty-stricken populations in various nations and concluded that access to adequate food, shelter, and health care is a basic human right often violated

Prober: How big is the military and how do they do their recruiting?

Spinner: I'm not sure about the size but I've heard it's many millions. They get some recruits by advertising the glory of killing and domination.[111] You saw the billboards as we drove in here. But that doesn't bring in enough because Emperor Ninny loves to start new wars and so do the executives of Apocalypse Industries. Consequently, they have to use some other recruiting methods. They draft a lot by going right into poor towns like Toxica and buying Putrid-Scum children from their parents. They also skim off a lot of very young kids directly from the schools: those who aren't doing well on the standardized tests. And if that still doesn't yield enough, they recruit from the prisons and the senior-citizen care homes. The prisoners in our Bastille Battalions, as we call them, are chained together in leg irons so they won't escape in the confusion of battle. But they make great soldiers because the leg irons force them to work in teams and, of course, they have nothing to lose. Our generals usually send the Bastille Battalions and the Grisly Grunts Senior Brigades into a war zone in the first wave of an invasion so the enemy will waste ammunition on them before we send in the elite troops The seniors will die soon anyway so this gives them a final chance to be heroic. You should see some of the weapons Homicidal Industries manufactures for the Grisly Grunts Senior Brigades! They have machine guns built into their walkers, rocket-launching wheelchairs, night-vision trifocals, and Kevlar armored adult diapers that stretch up to the armpits. Overall, the recruiting is very effective because the Army of the Apocalypse is the biggest employer in the nation by far.

Prober: Parents sell their kids to the military?! And you get recruits from the schools and seniors' rest homes?!

---

by our socioeconomic systems. Consequently, improving the life conditions of the world's poor is the most pressing human-rights issue of the 21st century. In America, racism and gender inequality are important aspects of this human-rights problem because they intensify and maintain the suffering of the deprived.

111 Fletcher (2002) reported the periodic ascendance of Romanticism in the public consciousness. After a period of intensive warfare, the horrors of battle tarnish the glory of conquest to the point where we regain our reason. These inhibitions last for several decades and then Romanticism ascends once again because new generations lack the horrific memories of past conflicts. In these periods of romantic resurgence, we are inclined to support war once again, even relishing it because we are caught up in the glory and excitement of grand causes. In these romantic periods, unscrupulous leaders easily can deceive the populace into supporting unjust wars.

Soldier in the Grisly Grunts Senior Brigade

Spinner: You saw how they live in Toxica. If you were a parent, wouldn't you want your kid to have a better life in the army?[112] And the educational failures go right out the back door of the schools because they're headed for Homeless Alley and then the prisons anyway. Since the Great Privatization, most seniors can't afford elder care so the army is a good option for them. And there's still one other way the military does its recruiting. If they're running short of the monthly quota, they use press gangs in places like Toxica.

112 Military recruiters target poor youth because they have very limited life opportunities and future prospects (Lipman, 2004).

Remember Trash Mountain? The recruiters wait at the bottom for the refuse pickers to come down at night and then they round up the most promising candidates, spray them down with a fire hose, chain them together and load them into buses.

Prober: Aren't press gangs illegal? Kidnapping and forcing people into service against their will just doesn't sound right.

Spinner: It worked really well for the British Navy in the 18th and early 19th centuries.

Prober: That was bad enough but they kidnapped only people between the ages of 18 and 55 with seafaring experience. And the captives had a right to appeal, which often worked in their favor. You're talking about forcing everyone into the military, including children. They're only kids!

Spinner: That's the best time to recruit them. Apocalypse Industries learned a lot from the Neoconland Chicanery Institute (NCI) fellows who studied military recruiting and service throughout history. Callous Bombast, the former 38-star general who now holds a senior fellowship at the NCI, discovered some useful strategies from historical records. In fact, he's the one who promoted the recruiting of children after he found out the Spartans of ancient Greece used to take young kids away from their parents and then abused them and raised them in harsh conditions to create a compliant yet aggressive and highly skilled army. Apocalypse Industries isn't doing anything that hasn't been done before. Let's continue the tour of the base. See that stadium over there?

Prober: Is that where the army plays football?

Spinner: On the weekends, yes. But during the week they use it for public executions of deserters and the public torture of war prisoners, something like the shows you saw back in the prison.

Prober: Come on, you can't possibly be serious.

Spinner: Think about it. What better way for Apocalypse Industries to keep the soldiers in line and to show the world it means business? This is another brainchild of the fishboys at the Neoconland Chicanery Institute think tank. Desertion rates are way down and the executions contribute to the complete dehumanization of soldiers in basic training, which needs to happen in order to create a compliant army willing to kill with abandon. And the torture sure keeps other nations fearful of us. Aside from that it makes for great family entertainment, just like in the medieval days. I tell you, when there are executions or torture events scheduled it's standing room only and a lot of ticket scalping goes on, pardon the pun. These events are top-rated prime-time shows on Weasel News. They're right up there with the televised public executions and gladiatorial combat at Wretched Warehouse Prison. You can't argue with success like that.

Spinner's words were drowned out by the deafening roar of fighter jets and bombers racing off to the northwest. Thousands of them darkened the sky like a gathering thunderstorm. Looking out to the harbor we could see legions of soldiers marching aboard hundreds of warships.[113]

Prober: What's happening?

Spinner: Oh, the CEO of Apocalypse Industries announced today that we would be invading Benignland, a small country out in the Vassal Lands.

Prober: For what reason? What did they do?

Spinner: What do you mean, reason? Apocalypse Industries doesn't need a reason anymore, not like in the old days when they had to tell about evil things the barbarians in the Vassal Lands must have done.[114] Everyone knows the leaders of Apocalypse Industries act only in our best interests and they protect and project the honor and glory of our nation.[115]

How could anyone possibly question their motives? That would be treasonous, not to mention a violation of the Corporate Protection Act. You're not questioning their motives, are you?

Prober: Oh no, of course not!

Spinner: I guess we're in the way here. Maybe we'd better move on to the airport. It's near time for your flight home.

---

113 Johnson (2004) described the widespread militarism of post-cold-war America, which rests upon the encouragement of pro-military decision makers in key government positions and entails enormous commitments of resources to sustain hundreds of expensive military bases around the world. Aside from the huge financial burden, which is nudging the nation toward bankruptcy, the extension of our military throughout the world is creating resentment and potential retaliation internationally.

114 We haven't come quite this far yet; however, radical neoconservatives did commandeer the government policy apparatus that enabled them to start preemptive wars and engage in nation building in foreign lands with the purpose of remaking important regions of the world in their own ideological image (Halper & Clark, 2004, Wolin, 2008). The costs in blood and money have been astronomical, particularly in Iraq. Other costs include weakened security, eroding civil liberties, and growing anti-Americanism around the world.

115 National glory is a dubious reason for warfare, especially when many nations tend to be bound up in self-exalting ideology. Glover (2000) showed how blind faith in an ideology combined with diminished personal responsibility and hatred of foreigners led to many of the most vicious, immoral conquests and genocides in the 20th century, which arguably was the most brutal era in human history. According to Weitz (2003), genocide often occurs when a strong state blindly following a utopian ideology identifies particular national or racial groups as enemies in need of domination or annihilation.

CH 16.

HEADING HOME FROM
CATTLE-PROD AIRPORT

The terrible storms between Neoconland and the Neutral Lands had subsided briefly so it was my good fortune to take a flight home instead of returning on a rolling ship in rough seas, or so I thought. I should have known by now that Cattle-Prod Airport, one more location named in the spirit of Cowboy Clod, would present yet another set of stress-inducing challenges. Cattle-Prod actually was two airports: a lavish, exclusive one for the Splendiferous Bluebloods and a few of the top Insatiable Predators and a confusing, teeming, grotty one for everyone else.

Spinner: Bet you wish you were a Blueblood, Mr. Prober. They follow a special road into the airport, pull their limos right onto the runway, step into their corporate jets, and take off in just a few minutes because they have customs and runway clearance priority. But you do pretty well if you get the triple platinum, gold-leaf, super-deluxe, elegant-premiere, blue-ribbon, five-star first-class tickets for the regular planes. Most Insatiable Predators ride in first class enjoying the king-size, vibrating, reclining seats, gourmet meals, massages, manicures, and live entertainment complete with a dance floor and a Jacuzzi. The rest of the passengers have to ride in rubbish class. Surprisingly, Charlatan Airlines makes the bulk of their profit from rubbish class because they took out the seats and installed handrails in the ceiling so they could pack many more customers in standing room only. They also took the restrooms out of that section to make even more space. And that brings in a little more money yet because they sell adult diapers at a big markup to any customers who think they can't hold it for a five-hour flight. If nothing else, you'll head home with a much deeper appreciation for the entrepreneurial spirit that makes Charlatan the most profitable airline in the world.

Prober: Unfortunately, my newspaper sprung for a rubbish class ticket so I guess I better buy some diapers. I'm glad you told me about that! Anyway, I really appreciate your help throughout this trip. It's been a real blast.

Spinner: Yeah, it has been fun. I should ask you, though, when you write your stories about the trip, you'll be fair, won't you? A few stupid, shortsighted people have criticized our ways in the past even though it's obvious to anyone with half a brain that our nation is the first and only genuine utopia in world history.

Prober: Oh yes, I'll make sure I give your nation its due.

Spinner dropped me off at the departure gate where I made my way through airport security. Lacking either a Splendiferous Blueblood or Insatiable Predator wrist tattoo, I was directed into a very long, slow-moving, high-security line where I was aggressively interviewed, strip-searched several times, and finally X-rayed.

After several, obligatory, storm-induced flight delays we were loaded into the dingy, windowless, littered, cavernous, rubbish class section of the plane. Screaming at us through megaphones and prodding us with, you guessed it, electric cattle prods, the flight attendants packed us into the back of the plane sardine-can style.

As I stretched up to grasp the ceiling-anchored handstrap a large, sweaty man pressed into my back while the oily hair of another fellow lubricated my chin. On my right, a screaming child sitting on his father's shoulders periodically jammed his dripping lollypop into my ear canal.

The cramped quarters thwarted my plans to review my notes in preparation for meetings with my editors back home. Nevertheless, thoughts were racing through my mind. What a fascinating trip this had been! As the Neoconians often say, there is no place like Neoconland. But how would my editors receive this story? Would they believe I really saw a child trading a slimy watermelon rind for a piece of rancid animal fat? Would they think I exaggerated about the size of Wretched Warehouse Prison or the Earth Devastator excessive egomobile vehicles? And how could I possibly get them to believe my descriptions of mind-crap-spewing, think-tank fishmen like Gil Flounderfib or psychopathic monkeymen like Hear No Warnings who regulate the work of scientists, or a giant, invisible hand curling into an iron fist and smashing players on a life-size game board? Fortunately, I had a lot of pictures that airport security neglected to confiscate. Everyone back home would get to see journalists like Pundit O. Gasbag and Shrilly Noxious, politicians like

Loading the Rubbish Class Section of a Charlatan Airlines Flight

Senator Hubris Mendacious III Esquire, and many other interesting people not to be found anywhere else on earth.

I also had one more ace up my sleeve, literally. About a week before my trip, an exiled Neoconian scientist had approached me with an unusual request when she heard I was about to set out for her homeland. Showing me a wrist-watch-like device she had invented, she asked me to do nothing more than wear it in place of my watch throughout the trip. When I pressed her on its purpose she told me it was her latest invention: a "thugometer," which could detect the core personality characteristics of anyone within a 50' range.

The technical details of its operation escaped me but the gauge was easy enough to read. The letters S, T, and F on the dial stood for scoundrel, thug, and fool. If the wearer pointed the watch face at someone, three lights would radiate outward from the rest spot at the bottom of the gauge to reveal the extent to which the individual was a scoundrel, thug, or fool. When fully lit, the sectors of the gauge registered the highest possible levels of scoundrel, thug, fool, or some combination. According to the scientist, the imperfection of humanity makes most people register a little of all three on the gauge. If a person truly is angelic, the lights hardly register at all. A cunning, deranged psychopath makes the scoundrel and thug lights radiate outward to the limits of the dial while leaving the fool section relatively unlit.

A well-intentioned idiot lights up the fool section of the dial but not the thug or scoundrel sections, and so on.

In my hotel room the night before the flight home I had docked the thugometer with my laptop computer to check its findings. To my surprise, a data table appeared registering STF scores for every person I had met on the trip. The scores ranged from 0-10 for each category with 0 signifying no discernible recording for a category and 10 signifying the highest possible score. Having time to read the scores of only a few Neoconians, I discovered the following profiles:

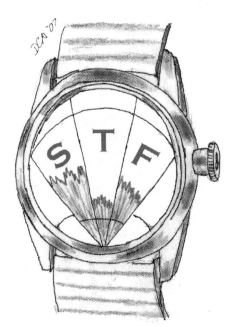

Thugometer: Wrist-Worn Personality Detector

Table 1 Thugometer Readout

NEOCONIAN	SCORES		
	SCOUNDREL	THUG	FOOL
Pundit O. Gasbag (news anchor; talk-show host)	2	10	10
Unearnest Merit III Esquire (heir to the Merit fortune)	1	1	10
Malign Lout (warden of Wretched Warehouse Prison)	5	10	3
Bovine Ninny (Emperor of Neoconland)	3	8	10
Senator Hubris Mendacious III Esquire	4	2	10
Shrilly Noxious (Weasel News reporter)	10	10	9
Abominate Frenzy (messianic cult leader)	10	6	2
Hear No Warnings (monkeyman scientific regulator)	0	8	10

I was very eager to see the other scores, and fearful of pointing the watch face at myself! After my editors had a chance to see the results of the thugometer along with my pictures, I was sure they would ask me to go back to Neoconland for a follow-up visit. What a great opportunity for a journalist. Nevertheless, exhausted as I was from this expedition, I pondered asking for an easier assignment next time—possibly the front lines of a foreign guerilla war.

Glossary of Characters

Note - Explanations of the names follow many of the entries. Those without explanations were considered to have obvious meanings not requiring elaboration.

Abominate Frenzy - messianic, fire and brimstone leader of the Maniacal Cult of Intolerant Absolutism. (abominate = loathing, detesting; frenzy = wild, maniacal)

Adam Smith - eminent 18th-century economist-philosopher who invented the invisible hand of the marketplace.

Atomistians - people from the town of Marketopia in Selfish Valley; obsessed with the materialistic game of Neoclassicon. (atomistic = reduced to a basic component part separated from all others)

Bimbo Jumbobazoom - famous heiress, socialite, and spokesperson for the bust-enhancing drug Elephanesta.

Bovine Ninny - the current Emperor of Neoconland; a man of very little brain but mucho charisma. (bovine = ignorant, witless; ninny = foolish)

Britney Bubblehead - perky, buxom Weasel News investigative reporter famous for breaking the story about a liberal politician's use of inappropriate colored nail polish.

Callous Bombast - former 38-star general; holds a senior fellowship at the Neoconland Chicanery Institute think tank. (callous = uncaring; bombast = pretentious bluster)

Cowboy Clod - first Emperor of Neoconland and former actor; iconic, god-like man of tiny intellect but massive charisma. (clod = stupid)

Facile Blinkerman - inventor of the Self-Infatuation and Traditional-Values Rear-View Mirror, or the Vainglory Mirror. (facile = simplistic, superficial; blinker = narrow, limited outlook)

Faux Oracle - leader of a think-tank group that discovered the Golden Slab. (faux = false; oracle = prophet)

General Blowhard Swagger - hero of the last battle in the first invasion of the Vassal Lands. (blowhard = loud windbag; swagger = arrogant, aggressive manner)

Gil Flounderfib - a human-fish hybrid who deposits ideological mind excrement in the bottom of neoconservative think tanks. (Gil and Flounder = his cold-blooded, fishman nature; fib = the lies that comprise the bulk of his mind excrement)

Hear No Warnings - monkeyman wearing corks in his ears; regulates scientific research by refusing to hear any criticism of corporate behavior.

Hidebound Flimflam III Esquire - a prominent fellow from the Neoconland Chicanery Institute think tank; author of the book *History: Done Like Dinner,* which inspired the building of the End of History Wall in the city of Fascisto. (hidebound = extremely conservative; flimflam = nonsensical, insincere communication)

Howler Frenzy - son of Abominate Frenzy and his heir apparent for leadership of the Maniacal Cult of Intolerant Absolutism.

Hubris Mendacious III Esquire - prominent senator with strong attachments to lobbyists for the Stupor Drug Pharmaceutical Corporation. (hubris = excessive, unjustified pride; dishonest)

Loopy Nefarious - televangelist who purchased the federal Department of Education during the Great Privatization to ensure the proper moral development of all children. (loopy = crazy; nefarious = depraved)

Malign Lout - warden of Wretched Warehouse Prison. (malign = evil, destructive; lout = ruffian)

Mountebank Ignominious - CEO of Box Kingdom Supermall and inventor of the profit-enhancing, molasses-filled pace clock. (mountebank = fraudulent, imposter; ignominious = disgraceful, shameful)

Noble Compassion and Livid Fairplay - liberal activists who regularly take a beating on Weasel News talk shows.

Patricia Plucky - promising journalist from the *Neutral Lands Gazette* who disappeared on an earlier trip to Neoconland. (plucky = courageous)

Peahead Lummox - country music star. (lummox = stupid oaf)

Pundit O. Gasbag - leading news anchor and talk-show host at Weasel News. (pundit = recognized as an expert regardless of worthiness; gasbag = full of hot air)

See No Progress - blindfolded apeman who regulates scientific research by blindly breaking up experiments that smell evil according to his moral sensibilities.

Shrilly Noxious - psychotic reporter and commentator employed by the Weasel News network; famous for making up stories about vile things the progressives might have done. (shrill = painfully loud; noxious = poisonous)

Slick N. Desperate - salesman working for Larceny Motors.

Speak No Sense - apeman who can speak fluently but thinks hardly at all while regulating scientific research; appointed to replace the Environmental Protection Agency administrator.

Spurious Rhetoric - lobbyist who wrote a book titled *Cool Times on a Hot Earth*, which promoted the benefits of global warming; not a real scientist, his academic background included a BA in duplicity with a minor in obfuscation from Dogma University. (spurious = false; rhetoric = persuasive language)

Starchy Supercilious - Headmaster of Hoity-Toity Château Chic prep school. (starchy = stiff, prim and proper; supercilious = pompous, conceited, condescending)

Unearnest Merit III Esquire - exalted lord of Merit Manor, which he inherited from his daddy Mercenary Merit; other famous Merits include Miserly Merit III, and Crony Nepotist Merit. (earnest = dedicated and thoughtful, so unearnest is the opposite; meritorious = worthy, eminent)

Wimpy Sham Radical - namby-pamby progressive who often appears as a guest on Weasel News shows. (wimpy = weakling; sham = fake)

Glossary of Locations, Organizations, and Artifacts

Affluenza Clothiers - upscale clothing store in Box Kingdom Supermall. (affluenza = psychological ailment of wealthy youth characterized by guilt, feelings of isolation, and lack of motivation)

Anti-Corruption Commission - government department ensuring fair and honest business operations; purchased and hamstrung by Fraudulent Finance during the Great Privatization.

Apocalypse Industries - largest military weapons manufacturer in the nation; purchased the National Department of Aggression during the great Privatization. (apocalypse = complete and final destruction of the world by violence)

Bastille Battalions - military units made up of fettered prisoners from Wretched Warehouse Prison. (Bastille = notorious prison of 18th-century France)

Beat My Bazooms - TV game show in which contestants compete for the largest drug-induced breast enhancement.

Bestial Shadow Agency - spies on all other secret police and spy organizations in the government to make sure they serve the interests of the Emperor. (bestial = savage, cruel, depraved, animalistic)

Big Boxica - commercial and financial hub of the nation; home of big-box superstores.

Bimbo Jumbobazoom Welfare Law - Legislation that made taxation of inheritances illegal; designed to protect the lifestyles of indolent, privileged children.

Boneshredder assault rifle - a favorite personal automatic weapon; grand prize at the Guns for Kids Jamboree.

Box Kingdom Supermall - largest shopping mall in the world, hotbed of consumerism, and the center of the materialistic universe.

Cattle-Prod Airport - the primary international airport serving Neoconland.

Chain Em Up: They're Useless Anyway - book written by Dr. Starchy Supercilious when he belonged to the Superficial Surface Skimming think tank; justified the deprofessionalization of public-school teachers, turning them into robot-like technocrats.

Charlatan Airlines - main passenger carrier in the nation; sells triple platinum, gold-leaf, super-deluxe, elegant-premiere, blue-ribbon, five-star first-class tickets, as well as rubbish-class tickets. (charlatan = a cheat, a fraud)

Citizen Monitoring Bureau - top-secret government agency that spies on most citizens in the country.

Civil Rights Building - a structure on Affirmative Action Boulevard in FDR Plaza; thought to be near completion but currently undergoing demolition.

compliance juice - powerful sedative extracted from the servitude tree; used to keep students compliant in lower-class schools.

Compulsory Commercial Gawking Act - requires all TV viewers to watch advertisements from start to finish under penalty of automatic fine.

Compulsory Firearm Totin' Law - requires every respectable citizen to carry a gun at all times.

corporate chain gangs - corporate use of free labor from Wretched Warehouse Prison; a business innovation that enhanced corporate profit.

Corporate Protection Act - law making it illegal to sue or criticize any corporation for any reason.

Coughing Coal-Black Industries - largest energy corporation in the land.

Daft Harbor - the port town near Fascisto. (daft = crazy)

Decrepit Reformist party - very weak opposition party in the federal senate; the only alternative to the Neoconian politicians.

Department of Aggression - formerly the National Department of Defense, re-named to reflect its true purpose.

Diehard Regressive - passenger liner that brought Seymour Prober to the port of Daft Harbor in Neoconland.

Dissent Suppression Forum (DSF) think tank - silences or smears anyone who criticizes Neoconian activities or ideology.

Dodger Awards - prestigious ceremony in which the most cunning corporations receive trophies for finding the best loopholes to avoid the few remaining government taxes and regulations.

Dogma University - elite, neocon university with indoctrination as its mission; replaced all public universities during the Great Privatization. (dogma = set of absolute, unquestioned beliefs)

Double High - Right-Wing Authoritarians who have leadership skills.

Earth Devastator - largest excessive egomobile in the world.

Elephanesta - breast-enhancing drug in pill form; replaced breast-implanting plastic surgery.

Empathy Gulf Valley – once idyllic, now polluted; contains Flaming Filth River and the urban centers of White City and Toxica.

End of History Wall - monument built across History Street in the capital city of Fascisto; commemorates the founding of the neocon utopia.

Environmental Loonie Law - sends environmentalists directly to prison without trial.

Excessive Egomobile (EEM) - next generation of SUV; largest private vehicles on earth; models include the Earth Devastator, Gold Star Ostentatiousmobile, Vainglorious Enviro-Buster, and Aggressive Belligerent.

Excessive Egomobile Deference Act - federal law requiring drivers to pull over to the roadside when an excessive egomobile is approaching.

Extermination Amphitheater – profit-generating public-execution wing of Wretched Warehouse Prison.

factory schools for the lower classes - provide assembly-line education for obedience and indoctrination; include Submission Elementary School, Indoctrination Middle School, and Resignation High School.

FDR Plaza - once vibrant but now crumbling set of progressive structures on the left side of Fascisto. (FDR = Franklin Delano Roosevelt, former American president famous for implementing highly successful social programs that alleviated unemployment and poverty)

Federal Assault Rifle Confederacy - powerful lobbying group promoting ownership and use of guns, the more lethal and widespread the better.

Flaming Filth River - polluted river in Empathy Gulf Valley.

Forget About Learning: Measure and Indoctrinate - book written by Dr. Starchy Supercilious when he belonged to the Superficial Surface Skimming think tank; initiated the standardized-testing accountability movement, which simplified and ratcheted down education for underprivileged children while cutting costs to the bone.

Fraudulent Finance - predatory lending high-interest loan and credit card company; purchased the federal Anti-Corruption Commission during the Great Privatization.

Glorious Birthright Foundation (GBF) think tank - protects privileged families from inheritance taxation while maintaining their control over financial institutions in the nation.

Golden Slab - stone tablet that replaced the old government constitution with a set of 10 directives; most important document on earth.

Great Deregulation - historical transition in which all government oversight of business and industry shut down; part of the Great Privatization.

Great Privatization - major event in Neoconian history; first Emperor sold off all government departments to corporations.

Great Sea - ocean separating Neoconland from foreigners in the Neutral Lands and Vassal Lands.

Grisly Grunt Senior Brigades - military units made up of senior citizens commandeered from retirement homes and assisted-living facilities. (grisly = horrific, disgusting; grunt = low-ranking soldier)

Guns for Kids Jamboree - monthly celebration featuring contests that put guns in kids' hands; jointly sponsored by the Federal Assault Rifle Confederacy, Homicidal Industries, and the Scrapburger fast-food chain.

Happyrefuse Company - garbage collection firm that keeps White City immaculate while expanding Toxica's Trash Mountain.

History Avenue - main drag of Fascisto, dividing the city into two sectors: a vibrant, growing right and a crumbling left.

Hoity-Toity Château Chic School - selective school for elite, Splendiferous Blueblood children. (Hoity-Toity = affluent and snobbish; Château = elegant castle; Chic = stylish, fashionable)

Homeless Alley - walled-off alley built by the government to keep homeless people off the streets away from respectable citizens; funnels the homeless into Wretched Warehouse Prison.

Homicidal Industries - largest of the nation's 14,218 gun manufacturers.

How and Where to Kick a Softie When He's Down - book authored by Shrilly Noxious; promotes extremist, right-wing political activism.

Hurricane Unnecessary - devastating storm induced by global warming; destroyed thousands of homes in Neoconland.

infobit pills - superficial knowledge in pill form poured into students crania through holes drilled into their skulls.

Insatiable Predator - highest socioeconomic class made up of egotistical, highly aggressive, self-aggrandizing materialists.

Invention Laboratory of the Federal Department of Stupor Drugs - lavish government scientific laboratory purchased by the Stupor Drug Corporation during the Great Privatization; carries out practical, pharmaceutical and cosmetic research on human subjects.

Kiddie Brigades - proposed addition to the national army to strengthen the invasion forces while promoting children's character development.

Larceny Motors - leading auto sales company. (larceny = theft)

Legacy Back Door Assessment - highly selective admission test for Hoity-Toity Château Chic school; subtest of the Myopic Standardized Test Battery; screens for appropriate family background and family contribution to the school's endowment.

Legacy Library in Dogma University - collects the genetic code of every citizen in the nation to enable efficient class distinctions and surveillance by secret police.

legal system - has two tracks, the Shoddy track for the lower classes and the Boutique-Zenith track for the affluent; lower-class defendants face Quick-and-Dirty or Rubber-Stamp judges.

Lobbyville - small city of buildings attached directly to the back of the Capitol Building in Fascisto; houses thousands of lobbyists who use puppet strings of threat and bribery to control politicians.

Loyal Lackey Tests - standardized tests for teacher employment screening; ensures hiring of loyal, malleable employees. (lackey = downtrodden, obedient servant)

Lucrative Hospital - best medical facility in the land; efficiently combines medical treatment with financial operations.

Lucre-buck dollar - official currency of Neoconland. (lucre = dishonorably acquired money)

Managing with Molasses and Other Great Ideas - book authored by management guru Mountebank Ignominious.

Maniacal Cult of Intolerant Absolutism - very aggressive politico-religious cult that destroyed the churches, synagogues, and mosques in the nation to become the sole official religious organization of the land.

Marketopia - town in Selfish Valley where the residents play the materialistic game of Neoclassicon.

Masters of Business Admiration (MBA) - popular degree earned at Dogma University; often preceded by Bachelor's degree in creative accounting.

Mindnumber Vacuous 3000 big-screen TV set - carries every form of entertainment on 17,000 channels; features the commercial tracking device, which scans the viewer's retina to ensure that he or she watches all advertisements from start to finish. (vacuous = empty, mindless)

molasses-filled pace clock - corporate innovation used to extract the most possible work from employees by extending the length of the work hour.

Mt. Exclusion - tallest mountain in the land; location of exclusive educational institutions.

MutantGene Inc. - most innovative genetic engineering company in the nation.

Myopic Standardized Tests - designed to assess superficial, factual knowledge from short-term memory; used for labeling children and teachers as miserable failures; designed and sold by the Superficial Surface Skimming think tank. (myopic = shortsighted)

National Community Media - declining media outlet formerly run by the government; the only competitor for Weasel News.

National Department of Basic Science Stuff and Miscellaneous Whatnots - underfunded, tightly monitored, government science laboratory where basic scientific research occurs under considerable harassment.

National Propaganda Ministry - government agency with the task of ensuring that important visitors see the true utopian nature of Neoconland.

National Science Institute - laboratories for research and scientific innovation; includes basic science and practical science departments.

Near Dregs - the lower working class.

Neoclassicon - materialistic game played by Atomistians in Selfish Valley; objective is to amass a bigger pile-o-treasure than anyone else.

Neoconian Baseball League (NBL) - professional sports league in the nation surpassed in popularity only by gladiatorial battles to the death at Wretched Warehouse Prison; teams are named after their corporate owners; most prominent teams include the Big Boxica Scrapburgers, Fascisto Assault Rifles, and White City Bling-Blingers.

Neoconland Chicanery Institute (NCI) - think tank employing positive spin to protect the Emperor and corporations from any embarrassment. (chicanery = underhanded, corrupt political action)

No Child Left Unscathed (NCLU) - federal law requiring all lower-class school students, regardless of ability, to be exactly average according to the rigorous Myopic Standardized Tests; punishes "failing" teachers and students with public humiliation.

Odious Thrash - top executive at a tanning factory in Toxica; graduate of Dogma University Masters in Business Admiration program. (odious = repulsive)

Organ Harvesting Lab - a profit-generating wing of Wretched Warehouse Prison where inmate's organs are harvested for medial transplants.

Ostentatious Jewelers - retailer noted for enormous pieces of jewelry. (ostentatious = pretentious, vulgar display of wealth and luxury)

Parochial Spinner - tourist guide from the National Propaganda Ministry. (parochial = narrow-minded; spin = propaganda)

Plutocracy - rule by and for the wealthy few; replaced democracy as the preferred form of government in Neoconland.

Pundit O. Gasbag show - top-rated news show on the Weasel News television network.

punishment zappers - high-voltage electric wires attached to students' fingers in lower-class schools; backup system to ensure obedience.

Putrid Scum - lowest socioeconomic class in the nation; considered despicable, exploitable, and expendable.

Rapscallion Corporation - purchased the public schools during the Great Privatization; owned by the televangelist Loopy Nefarious. (rapscallion = mischievous)

Recalcitrant vs. Frenzy - Zealots' court case about compulsory tri-weekly church attendance as a requirement of employment

Reprobate Intelligence Agency - top-top-secret government agency that spies on all the foreign Vassal Lands to select those most promising for invasion (reprobate = unprincipled, scoundrel)

Revisionist History Museum - a new building that will house artifacts glorifying the Neocon rise to power; will be built on the ruins of the demolished Civil Rights Building. (revisionist = changing memory of the past to fit a set of ideas)

Right-Wing Authoritarians - super-loyal and unquestioning yet aggressive followers of dogma.

Run 'Em Down and Snuff 'Em - TV show; special police unit hunts down and executes poor people who've had the audacity to appear in exclusive neighborhoods.

Savage Swine - super-super-secret, highly exclusive Dogma University society.

Scrapburger fast-food chain - distributes the Supersized Megaslopburger, the favorite food of the Near Dreg class.

Segregation Bridge - spans Flaming Filth River and separates affluent White City from impoverished, polluted Toxica.

Sentient Being Carve Up Laws - enable research and development laboratories to use animals and lower-class human subjects in any ways they see fit in efforts to discover profitable new drugs and cosmetics. (sentient = able to perceive or feel)

Seymour Prober - investigative journalist making a tour through the nation of Neoconland. (Seymour = able to "see more" than others; Prober = digs below the surface)

Skeptical Septic Tank (SST) think tank - trains its fellows to pretend they're scientists who refute complaints from environmentalists.

Slapdash Prize - most prestigious scientific research awards in Neoconland. (slapdash = careless)

Splendiferous Bluebloods - highest socioeconomic class; attained by birth privilege. (splendiferous = splendid, magnificent; blueblood = person of noble birth)

Stupor Drugs - largest pharmaceutical corporation in the land. (stupor = state of insensibility)

Superficial Surface Skimming (SSS) think tank - oversimplifies complex problems so politicians of minimal intellect look good when they suggest simple, black-and-white solutions for highly complicated issues; teaches its fellows to sound authoritative without having to be substantive or objective.

Taradiddle Times - oldest newspaper in Neoconland. (taradiddle = petty nonsense)

The 35 Worst, Evil, Demonic, Wacko Professors - book written by Dr. Starchy Supercilious when he belonged to the Superficial Surface Skimming think tank; contributed to the collapse of the old, public universities and the rise of Dogma University; encouraged replacement of intellectual college faculty with think-tank fellows.

Thugometer - wrist-worn device for detecting the core personality traits of people the wearer meets; assesses the degree to which the subject is a scoundrel, thug, fool, or a combination of these.

Toll sidewalks - built throughout the land to encourage pedestrians to drive excessive egomobiles.

Toxica - huge industrial, slum city built in swampland on the east bank of Flaming Filth River.

Trash Mountain - Toxican garbage dump, largest in the world; millions of Toxicans depend on it for their survival.

TriviaFacto Battery - backup admission test for Hoity-Toity Château Chic school; tests for superficial, short-term knowledge of fragmented facts.

Universal Health Care Hospital - a hospital that was under construction in FDR Plaza but wasn't completed before its demolition after the Great Privatization.

Vassal Lands - overseas foreign nations that the Neoconians regularly invade in search of resources and national glory. Altruistia and Benignland are two Vassal Land nations. (vassal = dependent subordinate)

Wartown - home of the military bases of Neoconland and launch point for invasions of the Vassal Lands; surrounded by the suburban towns of Slaughterville, Subjugatia, and Vanquishville.

Weasel News - dominant media outlet in Neoconland. (weasel = creepy scoundrel)

What Can You Eat? - TV show with contestants competing in eating contests to see who can scarf down the most disgusting things possible.

White Bulls of Revulsion - club for Right-Wing Authoritarians and Double Highs.

White City - affluent, exclusive suburban region on west bank of Flaming Filth River.

Worker Union Hall - building undergoing demolition in Fascisto's FDR Plaza.

Wretched Warehouse Prison - largest correctional facility in the world; employs innovative punishments and execution methods including gladiatorial combat.

wrist tattoos - designate an individual's socioeconomic class; applied at birth and used for employment screening and social exclusion.

Zealots' Court - highest court in the land comprised of nine judges who are owned and controlled by Neoconian corporate, political and cult leaders. (zealot = radical extremist)

References

Abernathy, S. F. (2005). *School choice and the future of American democracy*. Ann Arbor: University of Michigan Press.

Ackerman, B. A., & Alstott, A. (1999). *The stakeholder society*. New Haven, CT: Yale University Press.

Aho, J. (2006). Popular Christianity and political extremism in the United States. In D. M. Newman (Ed.), *Sociology: Exploring the architecture of everyday life* (6th ed., pp. 409-423). Thousand Oaks, CA: Pine Forge Press.

Altemeyer, B. (1996). *The authoritarian specter*. Cambridge, MA: Harvard University Press.

Altemeyer, B. (1999). To thine own self be untrue: Self-awareness in authoritarians. *North American Journal of Psychology, 1,* 157-164.

Altemeyer, B. (2004). Highly dominating, highly authoritarian personalities. *Journal of Social Psychology, 144,* 421-447.

Altemeyer, B., & Hunsberger, B. (2005). Fundamentalism and authoritarianism. In R. F. Paloutzian & C. L. Park (Eds.), *Handbook of the psychology of religion and spirituality* (pp. 378-393). New York: Guilford Press.

Ambrose, D. (1996). Turtle soup: Establishing innovation-friendly conditions for school reform. *Journal of Creative Behavior, 30,* 25-38.

Ambrose, D. (1998). Creative organizational vision building through collaborative visual-metaphorical thought. *The Journal of Creative Behavior, 32,* 229-243.

Ambrose, D. (2002). Socioeconomic stratification and its influences on talent development: Some interdisciplinary perspectives. *Gifted Child Quarterly, 46,* 170-180.

Ambrose, D. (2003). Barriers to aspiration development and self-fulfillment: Interdisciplinary insights for talent discovery. *Gifted Child Quarterly, 47,* 282-294.

Ambrose, D. (2005). Aspiration growth, talent development, and self-fulfillment in a context of democratic erosion. *Roeper Review, 28,* 11-19.

Ambrose, D. (2009). Morality and high ability: Navigating a landscape of altruism and malevolence. In D. Ambrose & T. L. Cross (Eds.), *Morality, ethics, and gifted minds* (pp. 49-71). New York: Springer.

Anderson, G. L. (1998). Toward authentic participation: Deconstructing the discourses of participatory reforms in education. *American Educational Research Journal, 35,* 571-603.

Apple, M. W. (2001). Markets, standards, teaching, and teacher education. *Journal of Teacher Education, 52,* 182-196.

Apple, M. W. (2004). *Ideology and curriculum* (3rd ed.). New York: Routledge.

Apple, M. W. (2005). Audit cultures, commodification, and class and race strategies in education. *Policy Futures in Education, 3,* 378-399.

Applebaum, R. P. (2005). Fighting sweatshops: Problems of enforcing global labor standards. In R. P. Appelbaum & W. I. Robinson (Eds.), *Critical globalization studies* (pp. 369-378). New York: Routledge.

Aureli, F., & de Waal, F. B. M. (Eds.). (2000). *Natural conflict resolution.* Berkeley: University of California Press.

Babb, S. (2001). *Managing Mexico: Economists from nationalism to neoliberalism.* Princeton, NJ: Princeton University Press.

Bacevich, A. J. (2002). *American empire: The realities and consequences of U.S. diplomacy.* Cambridge, MA: Harvard University Press.

Bacevich, A. J. (2005). *The new American militarism: How Americans are seduced by war.* New York: Oxford University Press.

Bakan, J. (2004). *The corporation: The pathological pursuit of profit and power.* New York: Simon & Schuster.

Baker, D. (2007). *The United States since 1980.* New York: Cambridge University Press.

Baker, W. E. (2005). *America's crisis of values: Reality and perception.* Princeton, NJ: Princeton University Press.

Bales, K. (1999). *Disposable people: New slavery in the global economy.* Berkeley: University of California Press.

Barlett, D. L., & Steele, J. B. (2002). *The great American tax dodge: How spiraling fraud and avoidance are killing fairness, destroying the income tax, and costing you.* Berkeley: University of California Press.

Berliner, D. C., & Biddle, B. J. (1995). *The manufactured crisis: Myths, fraud, and the attack on America's public schools.* Reading, MA: Addison-Wesley.

Bogle, J. C. (2005). *The battle for the soul of capitalism* New Haven, CT: Yale University Press.

Bohm, D. (1994). *Thought as a system.* London: Routledge.

Bowles, S., Durlauf, S. N., & Hoff, K. (Eds.). (2006). *Poverty traps.* Princeton, NJ: Princeton University Press.

Bracey, G. W. (1987). Measurement-driven instruction: Catchy phrase, dangerous practice. *Phi Delta Kappan, 68*(9), 683-686.

Bracey, G. W. (2002). *The war against America's public schools: Privatizing schools, commercializing education.* Boston: Allyn & Bacon.

Brandt, A. (2007). *The cigarette century: The rise, fall, and deadly persistence of the product that defined America*. New York: Basic Books.

Breit, W., & Ransom, R. L. (1998). *The academic scribblers* (Vol. 3rd). Princeton, NJ: Princeton University Press.

Bullard, R. D. (Ed.). (2005). *The quest for environmental justice: Human rights and the politics of pollution*. Berkeley: University of California Press.

Campbell, J. (1993). *Myths to live by*. New York: Penguin.

Chambers, S. (2002). A critical theory of civil society. In S. Chambers & W. Kymlicka (Eds.), *Alternative conceptions of civil society* (pp. 91-110). Princeton, NJ: Princeton University Press.

Chang, H. J. (2002). *Kicking away the ladder: Development strategy in historical perspective*. London: Anthem Press.

Cohen, L. M. (1994). Mode-switching strategies. In J. Edwards (Ed.), *Thinking: International, interdisciplinary perspectives* (pp. 230-240). Melbourne, Australia: Hawker Brownlow.

Cohen, L. M., Higgins, K. M., & Ambrose, D. (1999). Educators under siege: The killing of the teaching profession. *The Educational Forum, 63*, 127-137.

Coles, G. (2003). *Reading the naked truth: Literacy, legislation, and lies*. Portsmouth, NH: Heinemann.

Collings, B. A. (2001). *Words of fire: Independent journalists who challenge dictators, druglords, and other enemies of a free press*. New York: NYU Press.

Cross, J. R., & Cross, T. L. (2005). Social dominance, moral politics and gifted education. *Roeper Review, 28*, 21-29.

Cupit, G. (1997). *Justice as fittingness*. New York: Oxford University Press.

Currie, J. M. (2006). *The invisible safety net: Protecting the nation's poor children and families*. Princeton, NJ: Princeton University Press.

Davis, M. (2006). *Planet of slums*. New York: Verso.

Davis, S., & Meyer, C. (2000). *Future wealth*. Cambridge, MA: Harvard University Press.

Dayan, C. (2007). *The story of cruel and unusual*. Cambridge, MA: MIT Press.

de Waal, F. B. M. (2006). *Primates and philosophers: How morality evolved*. Princeton, NJ: Princeton University Press.

Dershowitz, A. M. (2002). *Supreme injustice: How the high court hijacked election 2000*. New York: Oxford University Press.

Diamond, J. (2004). *Collapse: How societies choose to fail or succeed*. New York: Viking.

Diebel, L. (2005). *Betrayed: The assassination of Digna Ochoa*. New York: HarperCollins.

Duncan, G. J., Yeung, W.-J. J., Brooks-Gunn, J., & Smith, J. (1998). How much does childhood poverty affect the life chances of children? *American Sociological Review, 64,* 406-423.

Edlin, G., & Golanty, E. (2006). *Health and wellness.* Boston: Jones & Bartlett.

Eisner, E. W. (1987). The celebration of thinking. *Educational Horizons, 66,* 24-29.

Eisner, E. W. (1993). The education of vision. *Educational Horizons, 71,* 80-85.

Eisner, E. W. (2001). What does it mean to say a school is doing well? *Phi Delta Kappan, 82*(5), 367-372.

Eisner, E. W. (2002). *The educational imagination.* Upper Saddle River, NJ: Merrill Prentice Hall.

Ensalaco, M. (2005). Pinochet: A study in impunity. In S. Nagy-Zekmi & F. Leiva (Eds.), *Democracy in Chile: The legacy of September 11, 1973* (pp. 116-129). Brighton, England: Sussex Academic Press.

Etzioni, A. (1993). *The spirit of community: Rights, responsibilities, and the communitarian agenda.* New York: Crown.

Etzioni, A. (2001). *Next: The road to the good society.* New York: Basic Books.

Fairbrother, P., & Griffin, G. (2002). *Changing prospects for trade unionism: Comparisons between six countries* London: Routledge.

Farmer, P. (2003). *Pathologies of power; Health, human rights, and the new war on the poor.* Berkeley: University of California Press.

Ferkiss, V., Bergmann, B., Agarwal, B., & Floro, M. (Eds.). (1993). *Nature, technology, and society: The cultural roots of the current environmental crisis.* New York: New York University Press.

Fischer, C. S., Hout, M., Jankowski, M. S., Lucas, S. R., Swidler, A., & Voss, K. (1996). *Inequality by design: Cracking the bell curve myth.* Princeton, NJ: Princeton University Press.

Flannery, T. (2006). *The weather makers: The history and future impact of climate change.* New York: Atlantic Monthly Press.

Fleischacker, S. (2004). *On Adam Smith's Wealth of Nations: A philosophical companion.* Princeton, NJ: Princeton University Press.

Fletcher, G. P. (2002). *Romantics at war: Glory and guilt in the age of terrorism.* Princeton, NJ: Princeton University Press.

Fukuyama, F. (1992). *The end of history and the last man.* New York: Avon.

Fullbrook, E. (Ed.). (2004). *A guide to what's wrong with economics.* London: Anthem Press.

Galbraith, J. K. (1967). *The new industrial state.* Boston: Houghton Mifflin.

Galbraith, J. K. (1996). *The good society.* New York: Houghton Mifflin.

Galbraith, J. K. (1997). The license for financial devastation. In J. H. Skolnick & E. Currie (Eds.), *Crisis in American institutions* (Vol. 10, pp. 86-93). New York: Addison-Wesley.

Gates, W. H., & Collins, C. (2004). *Wealth and our commonwealth: Why America should tax accumulated fortunes.* Boston: Beacon Press.

Gentile, E. (2006). *Politics as religion* (G. Staunton, Trans.). Princeton, NJ: Princeton University Press.

Giroux, H. A. (1999). Schools for sale: Public education, corporate culture, and the citizen-consumer. *The Educational Forum, 63,* 140-149.

Glover, J. (2000). *Humanity: A moral history of the twentieth century.* New Haven, CT: Yale University Press.

Goozner, M. (2005). *The $800 million pill: The truth behind the cost of new drugs.* Berkeley: University of California Press.

Graetz, M. J., & Shapiro, I. (2005). *Death by a thousand cuts: The fight over taxing inherited wealth.* Princeton, NJ: Princeton University Press.

Green, F. (2005). *Demanding work: The paradox of job quality in the affluent economy.* Princeton, NJ: Princeton University Press.

Gutmann, A. (2003). *Identity in democracy.* Princeton, NJ: Princeton University Press.

Habermas, J. (1996). *Between facts and norms: Contributions to a discourse theory of law and democracy.* Cambridge, MA: MIT Press.

Hacker, J. S., & Pierson, P. (2005). *Off center: The Republican revolution and the erosion of American democracy.* New Haven, CT: Yale University Press.

Hansen, J. E. (2005, December). *Is there still time to avoid 'dangerous anthropogenic interference' with global climate?* Paper presented at the American Geophysical Union, San Francisco.

Hawken, P. (1993). *The ecology of commerce.* New York: HarperCollins.

Hays, S. (2004). *Flat broke, with children.* New York: Oxford University Press.

Heilbroner, R. (1994). *21st century capitalism.* New York: W. W. Norton.

Herrera, S. (2004). Echo chamber of secrets: How science policy is being made by politicized science. *Acumen Journal of Life Sciences, 11,* 118-123.

Hochschild, J., & Scovronick, N. (2003). *The American dream and the public schools.* New York: Oxford University Press.

Hodgson, G. (2004). *More equal than others: America from Nixon to the new century.* Princeton, NJ: Princeton University Press.

Homer-Dixon, T. S. (2001). *Environment, scarcity, and violence.* Princeton, NJ: Princeton University Press.

Horowitz, D. (2006). *The professors: The 101 most dangerous academics in America*. Washington, DC: Regnery.

Howe, S. (2002). *Empire: A very short introduction*. New York: Oxford University Press.

Hughes, T. P. (2004). *Human-built world: How to think about technology and culture*. Chicago: University of Chicago Press.

Inglehart, R. (1997). *Modernization and postmodernization: Cultural, economic, and political change in 43 societies*. Princeton, NJ: Princeton University Press.

Inglehart, R. (2000). Globalization and Postmodern Values. *The Washington Quarterly, 23*, 215-228.

Institute of Medicine Committee on Assuring the Health of the Public in the 21st Century (2003). *The future of the public's health in the 21st century*. Washington, DC: National Academies Press.

Jacobson, M. (1997, September). For whom the gong tolls. *Natural History, 106*, 72-75.

Johnson, C. (2004). *The sorrows of empire: Militarism, secrecy, and the end of the republic*. New York: Metropolitan.

Kasser, T. (2002). *The high price of materialism*. Cambridge, MA: The MIT Press.

Katz, M. B. (1997). *Improving poor people: The welfare state, the "underclass," and urban schools as history*. Princeton, NJ: Princeton University Press.

Kessler-Harris, A. (2003). *Out to work: The history of wage-earning women in the United States*. New York: Oxford University Press (Original work published 1982).

Kinzer, S. (2003). *All the Shah's men: An American coup and the roots of Middle East terror*. New York: John Wiley and Sons.

Kinzer, S. (2006). *Overthrow: America's century of regime change from Hawaii to Iraq*. New York: Henry Holt.

Kirp, D. L. (2000). *Almost home: America's love-hate relationship with community*. Princeton, NJ: Princeton University Press.

Kivel, P. (2002). *Uprooting racism: How white people can work for racial justice* Gabriola, BC, Canada: New Society.

Klein, N. (2008). *The shock doctrine: The rise of disaster capitalism*. New York: Metropolitan.

Kohn, A. (2000). *The case against standardized testing: Raising the scores, ruining the schools*. Westport, CT: Heineman.

Kohn, A. (2001). Fighting the tests: A practical guide to rescuing our schools. *Phi Delta Kappan, 82*(5), 349-357.

Kornbluh, P. (Ed.). (2003). *The Pinochet file: A declassified dossier on atrocity and accountability.* New York: The New Press.

Kozol, J. (1991). *Savage inequalities: Children in America's schools.* New York: Crown.

Kozol, J. (1995). *Amazing grace: The lives of children and the conscience of a nation.* New York: Crown.

Kozol, J. (2005). *The shame of the nation: The restoration of apartheid schooling in America.* New York: Crown.

Krugman, P. (2004). *The great unraveling.* New York: W. W. Norton.

Kuttner, R. (1999). *Everything for sale: The virtues and limits of markets.* Chicago: University of Chicago Press.

Laird, P. W. (2006). *Pull: Networking and success since Benjamin Franklin.* Cambridge, MA: Harvard University Press.

Lakoff, G. (2002). *Moral politics: How liberals and conservatives think* (2nd ed.). Chicago: University of Chicago Press.

Lance, B. W., Lawrence, R. G., & Livingston, S. (2007). *When the press fails: Political power and the news media from Iraq to Katrina.* Chicago: University of Chicago Press.

Lasser, K. E., Himmelstein, D. U., & Woolhandler, S. (2006). Access to care, health status, and health disparities in the United States and Canada: Results of a cross-national population-based survey. *American Journal of Public Health, 96,* 1300-1307.

Lipman, P. (2004). *High stakes education: Inequality, globalization, and urban school reform.* New York: Routledge.

Lipsitz, G. (2000). Academic politics and social change. In J. Dean (Ed.), *Cultural studies and political theory* (pp. 80-93). Ithica, NY: Cornell University Press.

Loewen, J. W. (1995). *Lies my teacher told me: Everything your American history textbook got wrong.* New York: Touchstone.

Lott, B. (2002). Cognitive and behavioral distancing from the poor. *American Psychologist, 57,* 100-110.

Lubeck, S. (1995). Nation as context: Comparing child-care systems across nations. *Teachers College Record, 96,* 466-491.

MacLeod, J. (1994). Ain't no makin' it: Leveled aspirations in a low-income neighborhood. In D. B. Grusky (Ed.), *Social stratification: Class, race, and gender in sociological perspective.* Boulder, CO: Westview Press.

Marty, M. E., & Appleby, R. S. (1994). Conclusion: An interim report on a hypothetical family. In M. E. Marty & R. S. Appleby (Eds.), *Fundamentalism observed* (Vol. 1, pp. 814-842). Chicago: University of Chicago Press.

Massey, D. S. (2005). *Return of the "L" word: A liberal vision for the new century.* Princeton, NJ: Princeton University Press.

Massey, D. S., & Denton, N. (1998). *American apartheid: Segregation and the making of the underclass.* Cambridge, MA: Harvard University Press.

Mayer, D. (1998). Institutionalizing overconsumption. In L. Westra & P. H. Werhane (Eds.), (pp. 67-90). Lanham, MD: Rowman & Littlefield.

McCall, A. (1979). *The medieval underworld.* New York: Dorset Press.

McCally, M. (Ed.). (2002). *Life support: The environment and human health.* Cambridge, MA: MIT Press.

McKinnon, S. (2005). *Neo-liberal genetics: The myths and moral tales of evolutionary psychology.* Chicago: Prickly Paradigm Press.

McMurtry, J. (1999). *The cancer stage of capitalism.* London: Pluto Press.

McMurtry, J. (2002). *Value wars: The global market versus the life economy.* London: Pluto Press.

Meier, A. (2003). *Black earth: A journey through Russia after the fall.* New York: W. W. Norton.

Meier, D., & Wood, G. (Eds.). (2004). *Many children left behind: How the No Child Left Behind Act is damaging our children and our schools.* Boston: Beacon Press.

Meltzer, M. (1990). *Crime in America.* New York: Morrow Junior Books.

Mendelberg, T. (2001). *The race card: Campaign strategy, implicit messages, and the norm of equality.* Princeton, NJ: Princeton University Press.

Michaels, D. (2005, June). Doubt is their product. *Scientific American, 292,* 96-101.

Midgley, M. (2000). *Science and poetry.* London: Routledge.

Miller, A. I. (1986). *Imagery in scientific thought: Creating 20th-century physics.* Cambridge, MA: MIT Press.

Miller, A. I. (1989). Imagery and intuition in creative scientific thinking: Albert Einstein's invention of the special theory of relativity. In D. B. Wallace & H. E. Gruber (Eds.), *Creative people at work* (pp. 171-188). New York: Oxford University Press.

Miller, A. I. (1996). *Insights of genius: Imagery and creativity in science and art.* New York: Springer-Verlag.

Miller, M. C. (2004). *Cruel and unusual: Bush/Cheney's new world order.* New York: W. W. Norton.

Moffett, J. (1994). On to the past: Wrong-headed school reform. *Phi Delta Kappan, 75*(8), 584-590.

Monbiot, G. (2000). *Captive state: The corporate takeover of Britain.* London: Macmillan.

Moore, B., Jr. (2000). *Moral purity and persecution in history.* Princeton, NJ: Princeton University Press.

Morgan, K. P. (1994). Women and the knife: Cosmetic surgery and the colonization of women's bodies. In A. M. Jaggar (Ed.), *Living with contradictions: Controversies in feminist social ethics* (pp. 239-256). Boulder, CO: Westview Press.

Muller, J. Z. (1995). *Adam Smith in his time and ours: Designing the decent society.* Princeton, NJ: Princteon University Press.

Murphy, C. (2007). *Are we Rome? The fall of an empire and the fate of America.* New York: Houghton Mifflin.

Nadeau, R. L. (2003). *The wealth of nature: How mainstream economics has failed the environment.* New York: Columbia University Press.

Newfield, C., & Strickland, R. (Eds.). (1995). *After political correctness: The humanities and society in the 1990s.* Boulder, CO: Westview Press.

O'Connor, A. (2001). *Poverty knowledge: Social science, social policy, and the poor in twentieth-century U.S. history.* Princeton, NJ: Princteon University Press.

Oakes, J. (1986). *Keeping track: How schools structure inequality.* New Haven, CT: Yale University Press.

Ohanian, S. (2001). News from the test resistance trail. *Phi Delta Kappan, 82*(5), 363-366.

Orend, B. (2002). *Human rights: Concept and context.* Peterborough, Canada: Broadview Press.

Orlie, M. A. (2001). Political capitalism and the consumption of democracy. In A. Botwinick & W. E. Connolly (Eds.), *Democracy and vision: Sheldon Wolin and the vicissitudes of the political* (pp. 138-160). Princteon, NJ: Princeton University Press.

Pellow, D. N. (2002). *Garbage wars: The struggle for environmental justice in Chicago.* Cambridge, MA: MIT Press.

Pellow, D. N. (2007). *Resisting global toxics: Transnational movements for environmental justice.* Cambridge, MA: MIT Press.

Pérez, J. (2006). *The Spanish Inquisition: A history* (J. Lloyd, Trans.). New Haven, CT: Yale University Press.

Perrow, C. (2002). *Organizing America: Wealth, power, and the origins of corporate capitalism.* Princeton, NJ: Princeton University Press.

Phillips, K. (2002). *Wealth and democracy: A political history of the American rich.* New York: Broadway Books.

Price, D. P. T. (2000). *Legal and ethical aspects of organ transplantation.* Cambridge, England: Cambridge University Press.

Rainwater, L., & Smeeding, T. M. (2003). *Poor kids in a rich country: America's children in comparative perspective.* New York: Russel Sage Foundation.

Rapley, J. (2004). *Globalization and inequality: Neoliberalism's downward spiral.* Boulder, CO: Lynne Rienner.

Ravitch, D. (2000). *Left back: A century of failed school reforms.* New York: Simon & Schuster.

Ricci, B. D. M. (2004). *Good citizenship in America.* New York: Cambridge University Press.

Ringmar, E. (2005). *Surviving capitalism: How we learned to live with the market and remained almost human.* London: Anthem Press.

Robertson, H. J. (2001). The right to rights. *Phi Delta Kappan, 82*(9), 719-720.

Rose, M. R. (1998). *Darwin's spectre: Evolutionary biology in the modern world.* Princeton, NJ: Princeton University Press.

Sacks, P. (2007). *Tearing down the gates: Confronting the class divide in American education.* Berkeley: University of California Press.

Sandel, M. J. (2005). *Public philosophy: Essays on morality in politics.* Cambridge, MA: Harvard University Press.

Satter, D. (2003). *Darkness at dawn: The rise of the Russian criminal state.* New Haven, CT: Yale University Press.

Saul, J. R. (2005). *The collapse of globalism and the reinvention of the world.* New York: Overlook Press.

Scott, J. W. (2001). After history? In J. W. Scott & D. Keates (Eds.), *Schools of thought: Twenty-five years of interpretive social science* (pp. 85-103). Princeton, NJ: Princeton University Press.

Segal, J. M. (1999). *Graceful simplicity: The philosophy and politics of the alternative American dream.* Berkeley: University of California Press.

Sennett, R. (2005). *The culture of the new capitalism.* New Haven, CT: Yale University Press.

Shapiro, I. (2003). *The state of democratic theory.* Princeton, NJ: Princeton University Press.

Shiva, V. (2002). *Water wars: Privatization, pollution, and profit.* Cambridge, MA: South End Press.

Shulman, S. (2007). *Undermining science: Suppression and distortion in the Bush Administration.* Berkeley: University of California Press.

Sidanius, J., & Pratto, F. (2001). *Social dominance: An intergroup theory of social hierarchy and oppression.* New York: Cambridge University Press.

Sidel, V. W., & Levy, B. S. (2006). *Social injustice and public health.* New York: Oxford University Press.

Sizer, T. R. (1992). *Horace's school: Redesigning the American high school.* Boston, MA: Houghton Mifflin.

Skolnick, J. H. (1997). "Three strikes you're out" and other bad calls on crime. In J. H. Skolnick & E. Currie (Eds.), *Crisis in American institutions* (pp. 377-386). New York: HarperCollins.

Slaughter, S., & Leslie, L. L. (1997). *Academic capitalism: Politics, policies, and the entrepreneurial university.* Baltimore: Johns Hopkins University Press.

Smeeding, T., Rainwater, L., & Burtless, G. (2002). United States poverty in a cross-national context. In S. H. Danziger & R. H. Haveman (Eds.), *Understanding poverty* (pp. 162-189). Cambridge, MA: Harvard University Press.

Speth, J. G. (2004). *Red sky at morning: America and the crisis of the global environment.* New Haven, CT: Yale University Press.

Spring, J. (2002). *American education* (10th ed.). New York: McGraw-Hill.

Squires, G. D. (Ed.). (2004). *Why the poor pay more: How to stop predatory lending.* Westport, CT: Praeger/Greenwood.

Stark, R. (2003). *One true God.* Princeton, NJ: Princeton University Press.

Stefancic, J., & Delgado, R. (1996). *No mercy: How conservative think tanks and foundations changed America's social agenda.* Philadelphia: Temple University Press.

Sternberg, R. J. (2001). Why schools should teach for wisdom: The balance theory of wisdom in educational settings. *Educational Psychologist, 36,* 227-245.

Sternberg, R. J. (2005). WICS: A model of giftedness in leadership. *Roeper Review, 28,* 37-44.

Stivers, R. (2003). Ethical individualism and moral collectivism in America. *Humanitas, 16*(1), 56-73.

Strickland, D. H. (2003). *Saracens, demons, and Jews.* Princeton, NJ: Princeton University Press.

Suleiman, E. (2003). *Dismantling democratic states.* Princeton, NJ: Princeton University Press.

Sunstein, C. R. (2005). *Radicals in robes: Why extreme right-wing courts are wrong for America.* New York: Basic Books.

Symcox, L. (2002). *Whose history? The struggle for national standards in American classrooms.* New York: Teachers College Press.

Taylor, F. W. (1911). *The principles of scientific management.* New York: Harper & Row.

Thomas, M. D., & Bainbridge, W. L. (2001). All children can learn: Facts and fallacies. *Phi Delta Kappan, 82*(9), 660-662.

Thompson, S. (2001). The authentic standards movement and its evil twin. *Phi Delta Kappan, 82*(5), 358-362.

Veblen, T. (1994). *The theory of the leisure class*. New York: Penguin. (Original work published 1899)

Waligorski, C. P. (1997). *Liberal economics and democracy: Keynes, Galbraith, Thurow, and Reich*. Lawrence: University Press of Kansas.

Webb, S., & Webb, B. (1995). Inequality of income and inequality of personal freedom. In M. Desai (Ed.), *LSE on equality: A centenary anthology* (pp. 171-208). London: The London School of Economics and Political Science.

Weitz, E. D. (2003). *A century of genocide*. Princeton, NJ: Princeton University Press.

West, T. G. (1991). *In the mind's eye: Visual thinkers, gifted people with learning difficulties, computer images, and the ironies of creativity*. Buffalo, NY: Prometheus.

West, T. G. (2004). *Thinking like Einstein: Returning to our visual roots with the emerging revolution in computer information visualization*. Amherst, NY: Prometheus.

Westra, L., & Werhane, P. H. (Eds.). (1998). *The business of consumption*. Lanham, MD: Rowman & Littlefield.

Wilkinson, R. G. (2001). *Mind the gap: Hierarchies, health, and human evolution*. New Haven, CT: Yale University Press.

Willis, P. E. (1977). *Learning to labour: How working class kids get working class jobs*. Farnborough, England: Saxon House.

Wilson, E. O. (1978). *On human nature*. Cambridge, MA: Harvard University Press.

Wilson, E. O. (2002). *The future of life*. New York: Alfred A. Knopf.

Wolfe, A. (2006). *Does American democracy still work?* New Haven, CT: Yale University Press.

Wolin, S. (2004). *Politics and vision: Continuity and innovation in Western political thought* (Rev. ed.). Princeton, NJ: Princeton University Press. (Original work published 1960)

Wolin, S. (2008). *Democracy Inc.: Managed democracy and the specter of inverted totalitarianism*. Princeton, NJ: Princeton University Press.

Woodward, D., & Simms, A. (2006). *Growth isn't working: The unbalanced distribution of benefits and costs from economic growth*. London: New Economics Foundation.

Wuthnow, R. (2006). *American mythos: Why our best efforts to be a better nation fall short*. Princeton, NJ: Princeton University Press.

Xiang, B. (2007). *Global "body shopping": An Indian labor system in the information technology industry*. Princeton, NJ: Princeton University Press.

Yunus, M. (2003). *Banker to the poor: Micro-lending and the battle against world poverty.* New York: Public Affairs.

Zemelman, S., Daniels, H., & Hyde, A. (2005). *Best practice: Today's standards for teaching and learning in America's schools* (3rd ed.). Portsmouth, NH: Heinemann.

Zimring, F. E., & Hawkins, G. (1999). *Crime is not the problem: Lethal violence in America.* New York: Oxford University Press.

INDEX

imperialism, 7, 121-122
income, as unearned, 83
individualism, 20, 38. 50. 73-74
intellectuals, suppression of, 87-
    88
inverted totalitarianism, 31
journalism, 23, 112
judicial activism, 15
Gulliver's Travels, xi, xiii
labor unions, 8, 54, 68
lobbyists, 31, 55
medical system, American, 20,
    70, 119
merit, 46, 83, 96, 100
metaphor, and liberal or
    conservative ideology,
    101-102
microcredit, 77
military-industrial complex, 89,
    126
morality, particularist or
    universalist, 24
Nazis, 19
neoclassical economics, 15, 18-
    19, 21, 57, 68
Neoconservatives, xi-xii, 20-, 31,
    38, 45, 51, 57, 68, 77-
    78, 82, 96, 100-101, 126
neoliberal ideology, 16, 45
nuanced judgment, 28
organ harvesting, 115
patriotism, 24
pharmaceutical industry,
    and research
    and development, 69
Pinochet regime, of Chile, 12
Pol Pot regime, of Cambodia, 87

poverty:
    as a human rights issue, 122-
    123
    child, 20, 74, 78
predatory lending, 90
privatization, 6, 16, 20-21, 34,
    70, 89, 96, 101, 119
propaganda, xii, xiv, 2, 24
Romanticism, and grand causes,
    123
safety net, social, 51, 75
scientific management, 67
scientific research, as ideological,
    43, 87
segregation, racial and class, 73-
    74, 96
slavery, globalized, 68
Smith, Adam, xiv-xv, 55-59, 133
social Darwinism, 41, 46
social distancing, 27
social dominance, and right-
    wing-authoritarians, 110
Supreme Court, 15, 112
sweatshops, 68-69
tax cheating, 82
think tanks, xiii, xv, 37-42
torture, 112-113
trickle-down economics, 51
underground economies, 77
union busting, 54
universities:
    and legacy admissions, 104
    as market-oriented, 87
welfare reform, 75
women workers, as shock
    absorbers for the
    economy, 75
World Values surveys, 51